THIS IS YOUR **PASSBOOK**® FOR ...

ASSISTANT TRAIN DISPATCHER

NLC®

NATIONAL LEARNING CORPORATION®

passbooks.com

PASSBOOK® SERIES

THE *PASSBOOK® SERIES* has been created to prepare applicants and candidates for the ultimate academic battlefield – the examination room.

At some time in our lives, each and every one of us may be required to take an examination – for validation, matriculation, admission, qualification, registration, certification, or licensure.

Based on the assumption that every applicant or candidate has met the basic formal educational standards, has taken the required number of courses, and read the necessary texts, the *PASSBOOK® SERIES* furnishes the one special preparation which may assure passing with confidence, instead of failing with insecurity. Examination questions – together with answers – are furnished as the basic vehicle for study so that the mysteries of the examination and its compounding difficulties may be eliminated or diminished by a sure method.

This book is meant to help you pass your examination provided that you qualify and are serious in your objective.

The entire field is reviewed through the huge store of content information which is succinctly presented through a provocative and challenging approach – the question-and-answer method.

A climate of success is established by furnishing the correct answers at the end of each test.

You soon learn to recognize types of questions, forms of questions, and patterns of questioning. You may even begin to anticipate expected outcomes.

You perceive that many questions are repeated or adapted so that you can gain acute insights, which may enable you to score many sure points.

You learn how to confront new questions, or types of questions, and to attack them confidently and work out the correct answers.

You note objectives and emphases, and recognize pitfalls and dangers, so that you may make positive educational adjustments.

Moreover, you are kept fully informed in relation to new concepts, methods, practices, and directions in the field.

You discover that you arre actually taking the examination all the time: you are preparing for the examination by "taking" an examination, not by reading extraneous and/or supererogatory textbooks.

In short, this PASSBOOK®, used directedly, should be an important factor in helping you to pass your test.

ASSISTANT TRAIN DISPATCHER

Assistant Train Dispatchers, under general supervision, assist in dispatching trains in an assigned sector; electronically and manually check the times of arrival and departure of all trains, and record and maintain all related records. They enter departure and arrival times and names of crews and car numbers on train sheets; keep records of car mileage and of cars due for inspection; space trains; control train starting lights and bells; check traffic; act as crew dispatcher; maintain clear and meaningful communication with adjacent Gap points; prepare, maintain, check and file prescribed records; operate, when directed, interlocking plants and control points; may be required to crank switches and hook down stop arms and flag trains in emergencies; and perform related work.

EXAMPLES OF TYPICAL TASKS

Assists in directing the proper movement of all trains in the assigned territory, including supervision of the transportation employees concerned and the handling of unusual occurrences. Makes studies of traffic conditions, detentions, and adequacy of service; Keeps records of all train movements. Sees that transportation employees reporting in assigned territory are equipped and fit to perform their duties properly. Investigates accidents. Makes reports.

SCOPE OF THE EXAMINATION

The written test will be of the multiple-choice type and may include questions on: authority rules, regulations, and operating procedures; pertinent railroad terminology and equipment; car equipment capabilities from an operating viewpoint, signal aspects, and tower operations; supervision of subordinate personnel; various types of records and forms, such as train register sheets, which are pertinent to the duties of an Assistant Train Dispatcher; time tables and work programs; job-related calculations; emergency procedures; communication and safety on the tracks; written communication techniques; and other related areas.

HOW TO TAKE A TEST

I. YOU MUST PASS AN EXAMINATION

A. WHAT EVERY CANDIDATE SHOULD KNOW

Examination applicants often ask us for help in preparing for the written test. What can I study in advance? What kinds of questions will be asked? How will the test be given? How will the papers be graded?

As an applicant for a civil service examination, you may be wondering about some of these things. Our purpose here is to suggest effective methods of advance study and to describe civil service examinations.

Your chances for success on this examination can be increased if you know how to prepare. Those "pre-examination jitters" can be reduced if you know what to expect. You can even experience an adventure in good citizenship if you know why civil service exams are given.

B. WHY ARE CIVIL SERVICE EXAMINATIONS GIVEN?

Civil service examinations are important to you in two ways. As a citizen, you want public jobs filled by employees who know how to do their work. As a job seeker, you want a fair chance to compete for that job on an equal footing with other candidates. The best-known means of accomplishing this two-fold goal is the competitive examination.

Exams are widely publicized throughout the nation. They may be administered for jobs in federal, state, city, municipal, town or village governments or agencies.

Any citizen may apply, with some limitations, such as the age or residence of applicants. Your experience and education may be reviewed to see whether you meet the requirements for the particular examination. When these requirements exist, they are reasonable and applied consistently to all applicants. Thus, a competitive examination may cause you some uneasiness now, but it is your privilege and safeguard.

C. HOW ARE CIVIL SERVICE EXAMS DEVELOPED?

Examinations are carefully written by trained technicians who are specialists in the field known as "psychological measurement," in consultation with recognized authorities in the field of work that the test will cover. These experts recommend the subject matter areas or skills to be tested; only those knowledges or skills important to your success on the job are included. The most reliable books and source materials available are used as references. Together, the experts and technicians judge the difficulty level of the questions.

Test technicians know how to phrase questions so that the problem is clearly stated. Their ethics do not permit "trick" or "catch" questions. Questions may have been tried out on sample groups, or subjected to statistical analysis, to determine their usefulness.

Written tests are often used in combination with performance tests, ratings of training and experience, and oral interviews. All of these measures combine to form the best-known means of finding the right person for the right job.

II. HOW TO PASS THE WRITTEN TEST

A. NATURE OF THE EXAMINATION

To prepare intelligently for civil service examinations, you should know how they differ from school examinations you have taken. In school you were assigned certain definite pages to read or subjects to cover. The examination questions were quite detailed and usually emphasized memory. Civil service exams, on the other hand, try to discover your present ability to perform the duties of a position, plus your potentiality to learn these duties. In other words, a civil service exam attempts to predict how successful you will be. Questions cover such a broad area that they cannot be as minute and detailed as school exam questions.

In the public service similar kinds of work, or positions, are grouped together in one "class." This process is known as *position-classification*. All the positions in a class are paid according to the salary range for that class. One class title covers all of these positions, and they are all tested by the same examination.

B. FOUR BASIC STEPS

1) Study the announcement

How, then, can you know what subjects to study? Our best answer is: "Learn as much as possible about the class of positions for which you've applied." The exam will test the knowledge, skills and abilities needed to do the work.

Your most valuable source of information about the position you want is the official exam announcement. This announcement lists the training and experience qualifications. Check these standards and apply only if you come reasonably close to meeting them.

The brief description of the position in the examination announcement offers some clues to the subjects which will be tested. Think about the job itself. Review the duties in your mind. Can you perform them, or are there some in which you are rusty? Fill in the blank spots in your preparation.

Many jurisdictions preview the written test in the exam announcement by including a section called "Knowledge and Abilities Required," "Scope of the Examination," or some similar heading. Here you will find out specifically what fields will be tested.

2) Review your own background

Once you learn in general what the position is all about, and what you need to know to do the work, ask yourself which subjects you already know fairly well and which need improvement. You may wonder whether to concentrate on improving your strong areas or on building some background in your fields of weakness. When the announcement has specified "some knowledge" or "considerable knowledge," or has used adjectives like "beginning principles of…" or "advanced … methods," you can get a clue as to the number and difficulty of questions to be asked in any given field. More questions, and hence broader coverage, would be included for those subjects which are more important in the work. Now weigh your strengths and weaknesses against the job requirements and prepare accordingly.

3) Determine the level of the position

Another way to tell how intensively you should prepare is to understand the level of the job for which you are applying. Is it the entering level? In other words, is this the position in which beginners in a field of work are hired? Or is it an intermediate or advanced level? Sometimes this is indicated by such words as "Junior" or "Senior" in the class title. Other jurisdictions use Roman numerals to designate the level – Clerk I, Clerk II, for example. The word "Supervisor" sometimes appears in the title. If the level is not indicated by the title, check the description of duties. Will you be working under very close supervision, or will you have responsibility for independent decisions in this work?

4) Choose appropriate study materials

Now that you know the subjects to be examined and the relative amount of each subject to be covered, you can choose suitable study materials. For beginning level jobs, or even advanced ones, if you have a pronounced weakness in some aspect of your training, read a modern, standard textbook in that field. Be sure it is up to date and has general coverage. Such books are normally available at your library, and the librarian will be glad to help you locate one. For entry-level positions, questions of appropriate difficulty are chosen – neither highly advanced questions, nor those too simple. Such questions require careful thought but not advanced training.

If the position for which you are applying is technical or advanced, you will read more advanced, specialized material. If you are already familiar with the basic principles of your field, elementary textbooks would waste your time. Concentrate on advanced textbooks and technical periodicals. Think through the concepts and review difficult problems in your field.

These are all general sources. You can get more ideas on your own initiative, following these leads. For example, training manuals and publications of the government agency which employs workers in your field can be useful, particularly for technical and professional positions. A letter or visit to the government department involved may result in more specific study suggestions, and certainly will provide you with a more definite idea of the exact nature of the position you are seeking.

III. KINDS OF TESTS

Tests are used for purposes other than measuring knowledge and ability to perform specified duties. For some positions, it is equally important to test ability to make adjustments to new situations or to profit from training. In others, basic mental abilities not dependent on information are essential. Questions which test these things may not appear as pertinent to the duties of the position as those which test for knowledge and information. Yet they are often highly important parts of a fair examination. For very general questions, it is almost impossible to help you direct your study efforts. What we can do is to point out some of the more common of these general abilities needed in public service positions and describe some typical questions.

1) General information

Broad, general information has been found useful for predicting job success in some kinds of work. This is tested in a variety of ways, from vocabulary lists to questions about current events. Basic background in some field of work, such as sociology or economics, may be sampled in a group of questions. Often these are principles which have become familiar to most persons through exposure rather than through formal training. It is difficult to advise you how to study for these questions; being alert to the world around you is our best suggestion.

2) Verbal ability

An example of an ability needed in many positions is verbal or language ability. Verbal ability is, in brief, the ability to use and understand words. Vocabulary and grammar tests are typical measures of this ability. Reading comprehension or paragraph interpretation questions are common in many kinds of civil service tests. You are given a paragraph of written material and asked to find its central meaning.

3) Numerical ability

Number skills can be tested by the familiar arithmetic problem, by checking paired lists of numbers to see which are alike and which are different, or by interpreting charts and graphs. In the latter test, a graph may be printed in the test booklet which you are asked to use as the basis for answering questions.

4) Observation

A popular test for law-enforcement positions is the observation test. A picture is shown to you for several minutes, then taken away. Questions about the picture test your ability to observe both details and larger elements.

5) Following directions

In many positions in the public service, the employee must be able to carry out written instructions dependably and accurately. You may be given a chart with several columns, each column listing a variety of information. The questions require you to carry out directions involving the information given in the chart.

6) Skills and aptitudes

Performance tests effectively measure some manual skills and aptitudes. When the skill is one in which you are trained, such as typing or shorthand, you can practice. These tests are often very much like those given in business school or high school courses. For many of the other skills and aptitudes, however, no short-time preparation can be made. Skills and abilities natural to you or that you have developed throughout your lifetime are being tested.

Many of the general questions just described provide all the data needed to answer the questions and ask you to use your reasoning ability to find the answers. Your best preparation for these tests, as well as for tests of facts and ideas, is to be at your physical and mental best. You, no doubt, have your own methods of getting into an exam-taking mood and keeping "in shape." The next section lists some ideas on this subject.

IV. KINDS OF QUESTIONS

Only rarely is the "essay" question, which you answer in narrative form, used in civil service tests. Civil service tests are usually of the short-answer type. Full instructions for answering these questions will be given to you at the examination. But in case this is your first experience with short-answer questions and separate answer sheets, here is what you need to know:

1) Multiple-choice Questions

Most popular of the short-answer questions is the "multiple choice" or "best answer" question. It can be used, for example, to test for factual knowledge, ability to solve problems or judgment in meeting situations found at work.

A multiple-choice question is normally one of three types—

- It can begin with an incomplete statement followed by several possible endings. You are to find the one ending which *best* completes the statement, although some of the others may not be entirely wrong.
- It can also be a complete statement in the form of a question which is answered by choosing one of the statements listed.
- It can be in the form of a problem – again you select the best answer.

Here is an example of a multiple-choice question with a discussion which should give you some clues as to the method for choosing the right answer:

When an employee has a complaint about his assignment, the action which will *best* help him overcome his difficulty is to
  A. discuss his difficulty with his coworkers
  B. take the problem to the head of the organization
  C. take the problem to the person who gave him the assignment
  D. say nothing to anyone about his complaint

In answering this question, you should study each of the choices to find which is best. Consider choice "A" – Certainly an employee may discuss his complaint with fellow employees, but no change or improvement can result, and the complaint remains unresolved. Choice "B" is a poor choice since the head of the organization probably does not know what assignment you have been given, and taking your problem to him is known as "going over the head" of the supervisor. The supervisor, or person who made the assignment, is the person who can clarify it or correct any injustice. Choice "C" is, therefore, correct. To say nothing, as in choice "D," is unwise. Supervisors have and interest in knowing the problems employees are facing, and the employee is seeking a solution to his problem.

2) True/False Questions

The "true/false" or "right/wrong" form of question is sometimes used. Here a complete statement is given. Your job is to decide whether the statement is right or wrong.

SAMPLE: A roaming cell-phone call to a nearby city costs less than a non-roaming call to a distant city.

This statement is wrong, or false, since roaming calls are more expensive.

This is not a complete list of all possible question forms, although most of the others are variations of these common types. You will always get complete directions for answering questions. Be sure you understand *how* to mark your answers – ask questions until you do.

V. RECORDING YOUR ANSWERS

Computer terminals are used more and more today for many different kinds of exams.

For an examination with very few applicants, you may be told to record your answers in the test booklet itself. Separate answer sheets are much more common. If this separate answer sheet is to be scored by machine – and this is often the case – it is highly important that you mark your answers correctly in order to get credit.

An electronic scoring machine is often used in civil service offices because of the speed with which papers can be scored. Machine-scored answer sheets must be marked with a pencil, which will be given to you. This pencil has a high graphite content which responds to the electronic scoring machine. As a matter of fact, stray dots may register as answers, so do not let your pencil rest on the answer sheet while you are pondering the correct answer. Also, if your pencil lead breaks or is otherwise defective, ask for another.

Since the answer sheet will be dropped in a slot in the scoring machine, be careful not to bend the corners or get the paper crumpled.

The answer sheet normally has five vertical columns of numbers, with 30 numbers to a column. These numbers correspond to the question numbers in your test booklet. After each number, going across the page are four or five pairs of dotted lines. These short dotted lines have small letters or numbers above them. The first two pairs may also have a "T" or "F" above the letters. This indicates that the first two pairs only are to be used if the questions are of the true-false type. If the questions are multiple choice, disregard the "T" and "F" and pay attention only to the small letters or numbers.

Answer your questions in the manner of the sample that follows:

32. The largest city in the United States is
    A. Washington, D.C.
    B. New York City
    C. Chicago
    D. Detroit
    E. San Francisco

1) Choose the answer you think is best. (New York City is the largest, so "B" is correct.)
2) Find the row of dotted lines numbered the same as the question you are answering. (Find row number 32)
3) Find the pair of dotted lines corresponding to the answer. (Find the pair of lines under the mark "B.")
4) Make a solid black mark between the dotted lines.

VI. BEFORE THE TEST

Common sense will help you find procedures to follow to get ready for an examination. Too many of us, however, overlook these sensible measures. Indeed, nervousness and fatigue have been found to be the most serious reasons why applicants fail to do their best on civil service tests. Here is a list of reminders:

- Begin your preparation early – Don't wait until the last minute to go scurrying around for books and materials or to find out what the position is all about.
- Prepare continuously – An hour a night for a week is better than an all-night cram session. This has been definitely established. What is more, a night a week for a month will return better dividends than crowding your study into a shorter period of time.
- Locate the place of the exam – You have been sent a notice telling you when and where to report for the examination. If the location is in a different town or otherwise unfamiliar to you, it would be well to inquire the best route and learn something about the building.
- Relax the night before the test – Allow your mind to rest. Do not study at all that night. Plan some mild recreation or diversion; then go to bed early and get a good night's sleep.
- Get up early enough to make a leisurely trip to the place for the test – This way unforeseen events, traffic snarls, unfamiliar buildings, etc. will not upset you.
- Dress comfortably – A written test is not a fashion show. You will be known by number and not by name, so wear something comfortable.
- Leave excess paraphernalia at home – Shopping bags and odd bundles will get in your way. You need bring only the items mentioned in the official notice you received; usually everything you need is provided. Do not bring reference books to the exam. They will only confuse those last minutes and be taken away from you when in the test room.
- Arrive somewhat ahead of time – If because of transportation schedules you must get there very early, bring a newspaper or magazine to take your mind off yourself while waiting.
- Locate the examination room – When you have found the proper room, you will be directed to the seat or part of the room where you will sit. Sometimes you are given a sheet of instructions to read while you are waiting. Do not fill out any forms until you are told to do so; just read them and be prepared.
- Relax and prepare to listen to the instructions
- If you have any physical problem that may keep you from doing your best, be sure to tell the test administrator. If you are sick or in poor health, you really cannot do your best on the exam. You can come back and take the test some other time.

VII. AT THE TEST

The day of the test is here and you have the test booklet in your hand. The temptation to get going is very strong. Caution! There is more to success than knowing the right answers. You must know how to identify your papers and understand variations in the type of short-answer question used in this particular examination. Follow these suggestions for maximum results from your efforts:

1) Cooperate with the monitor

The test administrator has a duty to create a situation in which you can be as much at ease as possible. He will give instructions, tell you when to begin, check to see that you are marking your answer sheet correctly, and so on. He is not there to guard you, although he will see that your competitors do not take unfair advantage. He wants to help you do your best.

2) Listen to all instructions

Don't jump the gun! Wait until you understand all directions. In most civil service tests you get more time than you need to answer the questions. So don't be in a hurry. Read each word of instructions until you clearly understand the meaning. Study the examples, listen to all announcements and follow directions. Ask questions if you do not understand what to do.

3) Identify your papers

Civil service exams are usually identified by number only. You will be assigned a number; you must not put your name on your test papers. Be sure to copy your number correctly. Since more than one exam may be given, copy your exact examination title.

4) Plan your time

Unless you are told that a test is a "speed" or "rate of work" test, speed itself is usually not important. Time enough to answer all the questions will be provided, but this does not mean that you have all day. An overall time limit has been set. Divide the total time (in minutes) by the number of questions to determine the approximate time you have for each question.

5) Do not linger over difficult questions

If you come across a difficult question, mark it with a paper clip (useful to have along) and come back to it when you have been through the booklet. One caution if you do this – be sure to skip a number on your answer sheet as well. Check often to be sure that you have not lost your place and that you are marking in the row numbered the same as the question you are answering.

6) Read the questions

Be sure you know what the question asks! Many capable people are unsuccessful because they failed to *read* the questions correctly.

7) Answer all questions

Unless you have been instructed that a penalty will be deducted for incorrect answers, it is better to guess than to omit a question.

8) Speed tests

It is often better NOT to guess on speed tests. It has been found that on timed tests people are tempted to spend the last few seconds before time is called in marking answers at random – without even reading them – in the hope of picking up a few extra points. To discourage this practice, the instructions may warn you that your score will be "corrected" for guessing. That is, a penalty will be applied. The incorrect answers will be deducted from the correct ones, or some other penalty formula will be used.

9) Review your answers

If you finish before time is called, go back to the questions you guessed or omitted to give them further thought. Review other answers if you have time.

10) Return your test materials

If you are ready to leave before others have finished or time is called, take ALL your materials to the monitor and leave quietly. Never take any test material with you. The monitor can discover whose papers are not complete, and taking a test booklet may be grounds for disqualification.

VIII. EXAMINATION TECHNIQUES

1) Read the general instructions carefully. These are usually printed on the first page of the exam booklet. As a rule, these instructions refer to the timing of the examination; the fact that you should not start work until the signal and must stop work at a signal, etc. If there are any *special* instructions, such as a choice of questions to be answered, make sure that you note this instruction carefully.

2) When you are ready to start work on the examination, that is as soon as the signal has been given, read the instructions to each question booklet, underline any key words or phrases, such as *least, best, outline, describe* and the like. In this way you will tend to answer as requested rather than discover on reviewing your paper that you *listed without describing*, that you selected the *worst* choice rather than the *best* choice, etc.

3) If the examination is of the objective or multiple-choice type – that is, each question will also give a series of possible answers: A, B, C or D, and you are called upon to select the best answer and write the letter next to that answer on your answer paper – it is advisable to start answering each question in turn. There may be anywhere from 50 to 100 such questions in the three or four hours allotted and you can see how much time would be taken if you read through all the questions before beginning to answer any. Furthermore, if you come across a question or group of questions which you know would be difficult to answer, it would undoubtedly affect your handling of all the other questions.

4) If the examination is of the essay type and contains but a few questions, it is a moot point as to whether you should read all the questions before starting to answer any one. Of course, if you are given a choice – say five out of seven and the like – then it is essential to read all the questions so you can eliminate the two that are most difficult. If, however, you are asked to answer all the questions, there may be danger in trying to answer the easiest one first because you may find that you will spend too much time on it. The best technique is to answer the first question, then proceed to the second, etc.

5) Time your answers. Before the exam begins, write down the time it started, then add the time allowed for the examination and write down the time it must be completed, then divide the time available somewhat as follows:

- If 3-1/2 hours are allowed, that would be 210 minutes. If you have 80 objective-type questions, that would be an average of 2-1/2 minutes per question. Allow yourself no more than 2 minutes per question, or a total of 160 minutes, which will permit about 50 minutes to review.
- If for the time allotment of 210 minutes there are 7 essay questions to answer, that would average about 30 minutes a question. Give yourself only 25 minutes per question so that you have about 35 minutes to review.

6) The most important instruction is to *read each question* and make sure you know what is wanted. The second most important instruction is to *time yourself properly* so that you answer every question. The third most important instruction is to *answer every question*. Guess if you have to but include something for each question. Remember that you will receive no credit for a blank and will probably receive some credit if you write something in answer to an essay question. If you guess a letter – say "B" for a multiple-choice question – you may have guessed right. If you leave a blank as an answer to a multiple-choice question, the examiners may respect your feelings but it will not add a point to your score. Some exams may penalize you for wrong answers, so in such cases *only*, you may not want to guess unless you have some basis for your answer.

7) Suggestions
   a. Objective-type questions
      1. Examine the question booklet for proper sequence of pages and questions
      2. Read all instructions carefully
      3. Skip any question which seems too difficult; return to it after all other questions have been answered
      4. Apportion your time properly; do not spend too much time on any single question or group of questions
      5. Note and underline key words – *all, most, fewest, least, best, worst, same, opposite*, etc.
      6. Pay particular attention to negatives
      7. Note unusual option, e.g., unduly long, short, complex, different or similar in content to the body of the question
      8. Observe the use of "hedging" words – *probably, may, most likely*, etc.
      9. Make sure that your answer is put next to the same number as the question
      10. Do not second-guess unless you have good reason to believe the second answer is definitely more correct
      11. Cross out original answer if you decide another answer is more accurate; do not erase until you are ready to hand your paper in
      12. Answer all questions; guess unless instructed otherwise
      13. Leave time for review

   b. Essay questions
      1. Read each question carefully
      2. Determine exactly what is wanted. Underline key words or phrases.
      3. Decide on outline or paragraph answer

4. Include many different points and elements unless asked to develop any one or two points or elements
5. Show impartiality by giving pros and cons unless directed to select one side only
6. Make and write down any assumptions you find necessary to answer the questions
7. Watch your English, grammar, punctuation and choice of words
8. Time your answers; don't crowd material

8) Answering the essay question

Most essay questions can be answered by framing the specific response around several key words or ideas. Here are a few such key words or ideas:

M's: manpower, materials, methods, money, management
P's: purpose, program, policy, plan, procedure, practice, problems, pitfalls, personnel, public relations
   a. Six basic steps in handling problems:
      1. Preliminary plan and background development
      2. Collect information, data and facts
      3. Analyze and interpret information, data and facts
      4. Analyze and develop solutions as well as make recommendations
      5. Prepare report and sell recommendations
      6. Install recommendations and follow up effectiveness

   b. Pitfalls to avoid
      1. *Taking things for granted* – A statement of the situation does not necessarily imply that each of the elements is necessarily true; for example, a complaint may be invalid and biased so that all that can be taken for granted is that a complaint has been registered
      2. *Considering only one side of a situation* – Wherever possible, indicate several alternatives and then point out the reasons you selected the best one
      3. *Failing to indicate follow up* – Whenever your answer indicates action on your part, make certain that you will take proper follow-up action to see how successful your recommendations, procedures or actions turn out to be
      4. *Taking too long in answering any single question* – Remember to time your answers properly

IX. AFTER THE TEST

Scoring procedures differ in detail among civil service jurisdictions although the general principles are the same. Whether the papers are hand-scored or graded by machine we have described, they are nearly always graded by number. That is, the person who marks the paper knows only the number – never the name – of the applicant. Not until all the papers have been graded will they be matched with names. If other tests, such as training and experience or oral interview ratings have been given, scores will be combined. Different parts of the examination usually have different weights. For example, the written test might count 60 percent of the final grade, and a rating of training and experience 40 percent. In many jurisdictions, veterans will have a certain number of points added to their grades.

After the final grade has been determined, the names are placed in grade order and an eligible list is established. There are various methods for resolving ties between those who get the same final grade – probably the most common is to place first the name of the person whose application was received first. Job offers are made from the eligible list in the order the names appear on it. You will be notified of your grade and your rank as soon as all these computations have been made. This will be done as rapidly as possible.

People who are found to meet the requirements in the announcement are called "eligibles." Their names are put on a list of eligible candidates. An eligible's chances of getting a job depend on how high he stands on this list and how fast agencies are filling jobs from the list.

When a job is to be filled from a list of eligibles, the agency asks for the names of people on the list of eligibles for that job. When the civil service commission receives this request, it sends to the agency the names of the three people highest on this list. Or, if the job to be filled has specialized requirements, the office sends the agency the names of the top three persons who meet these requirements from the general list.

The appointing officer makes a choice from among the three people whose names were sent to him. If the selected person accepts the appointment, the names of the others are put back on the list to be considered for future openings.

That is the rule in hiring from all kinds of eligible lists, whether they are for typist, carpenter, chemist, or something else. For every vacancy, the appointing officer has his choice of any one of the top three eligibles on the list. This explains why the person whose name is on top of the list sometimes does not get an appointment when some of the persons lower on the list do. If the appointing officer chooses the second or third eligible, the No. 1 eligible does not get a job at once, but stays on the list until he is appointed or the list is terminated.

X. HOW TO PASS THE INTERVIEW TEST

The examination for which you applied requires an oral interview test. You have already taken the written test and you are now being called for the interview test – the final part of the formal examination.

You may think that it is not possible to prepare for an interview test and that there are no procedures to follow during an interview. Our purpose is to point out some things you can do in advance that will help you and some good rules to follow and pitfalls to avoid while you are being interviewed.

What is an interview supposed to test?

The written examination is designed to test the technical knowledge and competence of the candidate; the oral is designed to evaluate intangible qualities, not readily measured otherwise, and to establish a list showing the relative fitness of each candidate – as measured against his competitors – for the position sought. Scoring is not on the basis of "right" and "wrong," but on a sliding scale of values ranging from "not passable" to "outstanding." As a matter of fact, it is possible to achieve a relatively low score without a single "incorrect" answer because of evident weakness in the qualities being measured.

Occasionally, an examination may consist entirely of an oral test – either an individual or a group oral. In such cases, information is sought concerning the technical knowledges and abilities of the candidate, since there has been no written examination for this purpose. More commonly, however, an oral test is used to supplement a written examination.

Who conducts interviews?

The composition of oral boards varies among different jurisdictions. In nearly all, a representative of the personnel department serves as chairman. One of the members of the board may be a representative of the department in which the candidate would work. In some cases, "outside experts" are used, and, frequently, a businessman or some other representative of the general public is asked to serve. Labor and management or other special groups may be represented. The aim is to secure the services of experts in the appropriate field.

However the board is composed, it is a good idea (and not at all improper or unethical) to ascertain in advance of the interview who the members are and what groups they represent. When you are introduced to them, you will have some idea of their backgrounds and interests, and at least you will not stutter and stammer over their names.

What should be done before the interview?

While knowledge about the board members is useful and takes some of the surprise element out of the interview, there is other preparation which is more substantive. It *is* possible to prepare for an oral interview – in several ways:

1) Keep a copy of your application and review it carefully before the interview

This may be the only document before the oral board, and the starting point of the interview. Know what education and experience you have listed there, and the sequence and dates of all of it. Sometimes the board will ask you to review the highlights of your experience for them; you should not have to hem and haw doing it.

2) Study the class specification and the examination announcement

Usually, the oral board has one or both of these to guide them. The qualities, characteristics or knowledges required by the position sought are stated in these documents. They offer valuable clues as to the nature of the oral interview. For example, if the job involves supervisory responsibilities, the announcement will usually indicate that knowledge of modern supervisory methods and the qualifications of the candidate as a supervisor will be tested. If so, you can expect such questions, frequently in the form of a hypothetical situation which you are expected to solve. NEVER go into an oral without knowledge of the duties and responsibilities of the job you seek.

3) Think through each qualification required

Try to visualize the kind of questions you would ask if you were a board member. How well could you answer them? Try especially to appraise your own knowledge and background in each area, *measured against the job sought*, and identify any areas in which you are weak. Be critical and realistic – do not flatter yourself.

4) Do some general reading in areas in which you feel you may be weak

For example, if the job involves supervision and your past experience has NOT, some general reading in supervisory methods and practices, particularly in the field of human relations, might be useful. Do NOT study agency procedures or detailed manuals. The oral board will be testing your understanding and capacity, not your memory.

5) Get a good night's sleep and watch your general health and mental attitude

You will want a clear head at the interview. Take care of a cold or any other minor ailment, and of course, no hangovers.

What should be done on the day of the interview?

Now comes the day of the interview itself. Give yourself plenty of time to get there. Plan to arrive somewhat ahead of the scheduled time, particularly if your appointment is in the fore part of the day. If a previous candidate fails to appear, the board might be ready for you a bit early. By early afternoon an oral board is almost invariably behind schedule if there are many candidates, and you may have to wait. Take along a book or magazine to read, or your application to review, but leave any extraneous material in the waiting room when you go in for your interview. In any event, relax and compose yourself.

The matter of dress is important. The board is forming impressions about you – from your experience, your manners, your attitude, and your appearance. Give your personal appearance careful attention. Dress your best, but not your flashiest. Choose conservative, appropriate clothing, and be sure it is immaculate. This is a business interview, and your appearance should indicate that you regard it as such. Besides, being well groomed and properly dressed will help boost your confidence.

Sooner or later, someone will call your name and escort you into the interview room. *This is it.* From here on you are on your own. It is too late for any more preparation. But remember, you asked for this opportunity to prove your fitness, and you are here because your request was granted.

What happens when you go in?

The usual sequence of events will be as follows: The clerk (who is often the board stenographer) will introduce you to the chairman of the oral board, who will introduce you to the other members of the board. Acknowledge the introductions before you sit down. Do not be surprised if you find a microphone facing you or a stenotypist sitting by. Oral interviews are usually recorded in the event of an appeal or other review.

Usually the chairman of the board will open the interview by reviewing the highlights of your education and work experience from your application – primarily for the benefit of the other members of the board, as well as to get the material into the record. Do not interrupt or comment unless there is an error or significant misinterpretation; if that is the case, do not hesitate. But do not quibble about insignificant matters. Also, he will usually ask you some question about your education, experience or your present job – partly to get you to start talking and to establish the interviewing "rapport." He may start the actual questioning, or turn it over to one of the other members. Frequently, each member undertakes the questioning on a particular area, one in which he is perhaps most competent, so you can expect each member to participate in the examination. Because time is limited, you may also expect some rather abrupt switches in the direction the questioning takes, so do not be upset by it. Normally, a board member will not pursue a single line of questioning unless he discovers a particular strength or weakness.

After each member has participated, the chairman will usually ask whether any member has any further questions, then will ask you if you have anything you wish to add. Unless you are expecting this question, it may floor you. Worse, it may start you off on an extended, extemporaneous speech. The board is not usually seeking more information. The question is principally to offer you a last opportunity to present further qualifications or to indicate that you have nothing to add. So, if you feel that a significant qualification or characteristic has been overlooked, it is proper to point it out in a sentence or so. Do not compliment the board on the thoroughness of their examination – they have been sketchy, and you know it. If you wish, merely say, "No thank you, I have nothing further to add." This is a point where you can "talk yourself out" of a good impression or fail to present an important bit of information. Remember, *you close the interview yourself.*

The chairman will then say, "That is all, Mr. _____, thank you." Do not be startled; the interview is over, and quicker than you think. Thank him, gather your belongings and take your leave. Save your sigh of relief for the other side of the door.

How to put your best foot forward

Throughout this entire process, you may feel that the board individually and collectively is trying to pierce your defenses, seek out your hidden weaknesses and embarrass and confuse you. Actually, this is not true. They are obliged to make an appraisal of your qualifications for the job you are seeking, and they want to see you in your best light. Remember, they must interview all candidates and a non-cooperative candidate may become a failure in spite of their best efforts to bring out his qualifications. Here are 15 suggestions that will help you:

1) Be natural – Keep your attitude confident, not cocky

If you are not confident that you can do the job, do not expect the board to be. Do not apologize for your weaknesses, try to bring out your strong points. The board is interested in a positive, not negative, presentation. Cockiness will antagonize any board member and make him wonder if you are covering up a weakness by a false show of strength.

2) Get comfortable, but don't lounge or sprawl

Sit erectly but not stiffly. A careless posture may lead the board to conclude that you are careless in other things, or at least that you are not impressed by the importance of the occasion. Either conclusion is natural, even if incorrect. Do not fuss with your clothing, a pencil or an ashtray. Your hands may occasionally be useful to emphasize a point; do not let them become a point of distraction.

3) Do not wisecrack or make small talk

This is a serious situation, and your attitude should show that you consider it as such. Further, the time of the board is limited – they do not want to waste it, and neither should you.

4) Do not exaggerate your experience or abilities

In the first place, from information in the application or other interviews and sources, the board may know more about you than you think. Secondly, you probably will not get away with it. An experienced board is rather adept at spotting such a situation, so do not take the chance.

5) If you know a board member, do not make a point of it, yet do not hide it

    Certainly you are not fooling him, and probably not the other members of the board. Do not try to take advantage of your acquaintanceship – it will probably do you little good.

6) Do not dominate the interview

    Let the board do that. They will give you the clues – do not assume that you have to do all the talking. Realize that the board has a number of questions to ask you, and do not try to take up all the interview time by showing off your extensive knowledge of the answer to the first one.

7) Be attentive

    You only have 20 minutes or so, and you should keep your attention at its sharpest throughout. When a member is addressing a problem or question to you, give him your undivided attention. Address your reply principally to him, but do not exclude the other board members.

8) Do not interrupt

    A board member may be stating a problem for you to analyze. He will ask you a question when the time comes. Let him state the problem, and wait for the question.

9) Make sure you understand the question

    Do not try to answer until you are sure what the question is. If it is not clear, restate it in your own words or ask the board member to clarify it for you. However, do not haggle about minor elements.

10) Reply promptly but not hastily

    A common entry on oral board rating sheets is "candidate responded readily," or "candidate hesitated in replies." Respond as promptly and quickly as you can, but do not jump to a hasty, ill-considered answer.

11) Do not be peremptory in your answers

    A brief answer is proper – but do not fire your answer back. That is a losing game from your point of view. The board member can probably ask questions much faster than you can answer them.

12) Do not try to create the answer you think the board member wants

    He is interested in what kind of mind you have and how it works – not in playing games. Furthermore, he can usually spot this practice and will actually grade you down on it.

13) Do not switch sides in your reply merely to agree with a board member

    Frequently, a member will take a contrary position merely to draw you out and to see if you are willing and able to defend your point of view. Do not start a debate, yet do not surrender a good position. If a position is worth taking, it is worth defending.

14) Do not be afraid to admit an error in judgment if you are shown to be wrong

  The board knows that you are forced to reply without any opportunity for careful consideration. Your answer may be demonstrably wrong. If so, admit it and get on with the interview.

15) Do not dwell at length on your present job

  The opening question may relate to your present assignment. Answer the question but do not go into an extended discussion. You are being examined for a *new* job, not your present one. As a matter of fact, try to phrase ALL your answers in terms of the job for which you are being examined.

Basis of Rating

  Probably you will forget most of these "do's" and "don'ts" when you walk into the oral interview room. Even remembering them all will not ensure you a passing grade. Perhaps you did not have the qualifications in the first place. But remembering them will help you to put your best foot forward, without treading on the toes of the board members.

  Rumor and popular opinion to the contrary notwithstanding, an oral board wants you to make the best appearance possible. They know you are under pressure – but they also want to see how you respond to it as a guide to what your reaction would be under the pressures of the job you seek. They will be influenced by the degree of poise you display, the personal traits you show and the manner in which you respond.

ABOUT THIS BOOK

  This book contains tests divided into Examination Sections. Go through each test, answering every question in the margin. At the end of each test look at the answer key and check your answers. On the ones you got wrong, look at the right answer choice and learn. Do not fill in the answers first. Do not memorize the questions and answers, but understand the answer and principles involved. On your test, the questions will likely be different from the samples. Questions are changed and new ones added. If you understand these past questions you should have success with any changes that arise. Tests may consist of several types of questions. We have additional books on each subject should more study be advisable or necessary for you. Finally, the more you study, the better prepared you will be. This book is intended to be the last thing you study before you walk into the examination room. Prior study of relevant texts is also recommended. NLC publishes some of these in our Fundamental Series. Knowledge and good sense are important factors in passing your exam. Good luck also helps. So now study this Passbook, absorb the material contained within and take that knowledge into the examination. Then do your best to pass that exam.

———

EXAMINATION SECTION

EXAMINATION SECTION
TEST 1

DIRECTIONS: Each question or incomplete statement is followed by several suggested answers or completions. Select the one that BEST answers the question or completes the statement. *PRINT THE LETTER OF THE CORRECT ANSWER IN THE SPACE AT THE RIGHT.*

1. A flexible interval originates from

   A. gap points only
   C. a terminal only
   B. a tower
   D. gap points or terminals

   1.____

2. The terminal crew book is prepared from information contained in the train

   A. register sheet and train schedule
   B. schedule and work programs
   C. schedule and disposition sheet
   D. register sheet and work programs

   2.____

3. The type of track that has wooden ties bedded in stone ballast is Type

   A. I   B. II   C. III   D. V

   3.____

4. If a motorman is required to insulate a subway car from the third rail, he should use a

   A. frog
   C. housetop
   B. contact shoe slipper
   D. fibre tie pad

   4.____

5. Gap sheets are sometimes maintained by

   A. conductors assigned to platform duty
   B. motormen
   C. towermen
   D. yardmasters

   5.____

6. In a river tunnel, a train should NOT go faster than _____ mph.

   A. 15   B. 25   C. 35   D. 45

   6.____

7. When sound-powered telephones are being used by a train crew in an emergency, it is IMPORTANT to establish positive communication by

   A. constant voice communication
   B. speaking in a convincing voice
   C. responding immediately to orders
   D. using flashlight signals

   7.____

8. After an assistant train dispatcher operates an emergency alarm box, he should call

   A. the power department
   B. the transit authority police
   C. his immediate supervisor
   D. the command center

   8.____

9. A *No Clearance* area should be indicated by a sign painted   9._____

    A. red
    B. with red and white stripes
    C. with yellow and white stripes
    D. yellow

10. A certain motorman reports for work at 8 A.M. on Tuesday and normally clears at 3:30   10._____
P.M. He is paid at the hourly rate of $17.70.
What should his GROSS pay be for this day if, due to a train delay, he gets only 10
minutes for lunch?

    A. $141.60   B. $150.45   C. $156.30   D. $159.30

11. If a conductor works an 8-hour shift on his regular day off and it is a holiday, he should   11._____
get paid for _____ hours.

    A. 16   B. 18   C. 20   D. 24

12. The MINIMUM number of hours a motorman should get paid for working a *special* is   12._____
_____ hour(s).

    A. 1   B. 2   C. $4\frac{1}{2}$ D. 8

13. A certain towerman reports for work at 8 A.M. on Tuesday and normally clears at 3:30   13._____
P.M. He is paid at the hourly rate of $18.60.
What is his GROSS pay for this day if he is required to write an unusual occurrence
report at the end of his run?

    A. $148.80   B. $158.10   C. $165.60   D. $176.10

14. A motorman reports for work at 7 A.M. on a Tuesday and normally clears at 2:30 P.M. He   14._____
is paid at the hourly rate of $19.20.
What is his GROSS pay for this day is he has a student motorman with him?

    A. $153.60   B. $172.80   C. $192.00   D. $210.00

15. A certain conductor reports at 8 A.M. and normally clears at 3 P.M. His hourly rate of pay   15._____
is $16.50.
What should his GROSS pay be for this day if he is late at the end of his run and clears
at 4 P.M.?

    A. $132.00   B. $138.75   C. $148.50   D. $153.75

16. Providing the operating personnel for *extra trains* is the responsibility of the   16._____

    A. desk trainmaster   B. yardmaster
    C. motorman instructor   D. crew dispatcher

17. The train breakdown which will probably cause the LONGEST delay to a 10-car train is a   17._____

    A. side door that does not close
    B. blown main fuse
    C. grounded shoe beam
    D. defective motorman's indication

18. On work trains, the colors of the marker lights displayed at the front of the train should be   18._____

    A. yellow - yellow   B. green - green
    C. red - red   D. green - yellow

Questions 19-26.

DIRECTIONS: Questions 19 through 26 are based on the DAILY TRAIN SCHEDULE shown below. Refer to this schedule when answering these questions. Assume that all operations proceed without delay unless otherwise stated in a question.

DAILY TRAIN SCHEDULE
Q EXPRESS

SOUTHBOUND							NORTHBOUND			
Bar St.	St.	Love St.	Tom St.	Ann St.	Bell	Ave.	Ann St.	Tom St.	Love St.	Bar St.
ARR	LV	LV	LV	LV	ARR	LV	LV	LV	LV	ARR
710	720	726	734	744	748	754	758	808	816	822
P	730	736	744	754	758	804	808	818	826	832
730	740	746	754	804	808	814	818	828	836	842
P	748	754	802	812	816	822	826	836	844	850
750	756	802	810	820	824	830	834	844	852	900
P	804	810	818	828	832	838	842	852	900	908
804	810	816	824	834	838	844	848	858	906	914
810	816	822	830	840	844	850	854	904	912	920
P	822	828	836	846	850	856	900	910	918	926
816	826	832	842	850	854	900	904	914	922	930L
822	830	836	846	854	858	904	908	918	926	934
832	836	842	852	900	904	910	914	924	932	940
P	842	848	858	906	910	916	920	930	938	946

19. A passenger arrives at Bar Street at 812. He takes the next train leaving Bar Street to Bell Avenue. If he stays on this train, he will return to Bar Street at   19._____

    A. 816   B. 914   C. 920   D. 926

20. For the time period shown on the schedule, the number of trains placed in service at Bar Street which make one trip and then lay up is   20._____

    A. 0   B. 1   C. 2   D. 3

21. The smallest headway for trains leaving Bar Street for the period shown on the schedule is _____ minutes.   21._____

    A. 2   B. 4   C. 6   D. 8

22. A motorman leaves Bar Street with the 804 train. The amount of time required to travel to Bell Avenue and back to Bar Street is _____ minutes.   22._____

    A. 56   B. 64   C. 68   D. 70

23. The train that leaves Bar Street at 720 will on the next trip leave Bar Street at   23._____

    A. 730   B. 816   C. 822   D. 830

24. The total number of trains stopping at Tom Street between 822 and 838 is   24._____

    A. 2   B. 3   C. 4   D. 5

25. The southbound train leaving Ann Street at 854 should be followed by the train which left Bar Street at   25.____

    A. 822   B. 836   C. 846   D. 900

26. The length of time the southbound train which left Love Street at 746 spends at Bell Avenue is _____ minutes.   26.____

    A. 6   B. 8   C. 10   D. 12

27. The distance between signal B1-1052 and B1-1062 is APPROXIMATELY _____ feet.   27.____

    A. 10   B. 100   C. 1,000   D. 10,000

28. In the radio code signal system, a "12-3" means there is   28.____

    A. a train derailment
    B. a passenger under the train
    C. a flood condition
    D. fire or smoke

29. In the radio code signal system, a "12-2" means there is   29.____

    A. a stalled train
    B. fire or smoke
    C. an unauthorized person on the track
    D. serious vandalism

30. Traffic checkers usually have the civil service title of   30.____

    A. Assistant Train Dispatcher
    B. Train Dispatcher
    C. Schedule Maker
    D. Motorman or Train Operator

KEY (CORRECT ANSWERS)

1.	C	16.	D
2.	B	17.	C
3.	A	18.	C
4.	B	19.	C
5.	C	20.	A
6.	C	21.	B
7.	A	22.	B
8.	D	23.	D
9.	B	24.	D
10.	B	25.	B
11.	C	26.	A
12.	C	27.	C
13.	B	28.	C
14.	A	29.	B
15.	A	30.	A

———

TEST 2

DIRECTIONS: Each question or incomplete statement is followed by several suggested answers or completions. Select the one that BEST answers the question or completes the statement. *PRINT THE LETTER OF THE CORRECT ANSWER IN THE SPACE AT THE RIGHT.*

1.   In an emergency, an assistant train dispatcher may be required to   1.____

   A.   hook down stop arms and flag trains
   B.   operate the doors of a train
   C.   give out block tickets
   D.   supervise motorman instructors

2.   If a conductor finds any defect in a subway car, he must enter the information on the   2.____
   _____ sheet.

   A.   crew   B.   train register
   C.   car defect   D.   disposition

3.   According to the latest standard flagging instructions, the color of the lamp that should be   3.____
   used to indicate to the motorman to proceed very slowly and that there is a flagman
   beyond is

   A.   green   B.   blue   C.   yellow   D.   white

Questions 4-6.

DIRECTIONS: Questions 4 through 6 are based on the portion of a train register sheet shown
                       below.
MOTOR OR TRAIN CAR NUMBERS

1	2	3	4	5	6	7	8	9	10
3460	461	476	477	478	479	480	481	482	483

4.   According to the train register sheet, car number 3460   4.____

   A.   has been cut from service
   B.   has been added to service
   C.   is a bad order car
   D.   has brake trouble

5.   According to the train register sheet, car number 3481   5.____

   A.   is a bad order car
   B.   has been cut from service
   C.   has been added to service
   D.   is due for inspection

6.   According to the train register sheet, car number 3483   6.____

   A.   is a bad order car
   B.   has been added to service
   C.   is due for inspection
   D.   has been cut from service

7. Train register sheets are used MOSTLY at

    A. gap stations
    B. the central crew dispatcher's office
    C. the command center
    D. terminals

    7.____

8. A train register sheet usually does NOT include the

    A. point of origin of the train
    B. scheduled arrival time of the train
    C. motorman's reporting time
    D. actual arrival time of the train

    8.____

9. On a train register sheet, the symbol for a light train is

    A. LI   B. LT   C. L   D. BO

    9.____

10. A motorman loses his indication while his train is between terminals. The conductor has indication in both sections of the train and there are no guard lights lighted, and all side doors are closed and locked.
Which course of action should the motorman take?

    A. Keep the train in passenger service until it reaches the terminal, but only if a car inspector is aboard
    B. Take the train out of passenger service at the nearest station
    C. Keep the train in passenger service until it reaches the terminal
    D. Keep the train in passenger service only if a motorman instructor is aboard

    10.____

11. If a passenger train arrives ahead of time, the assistant train dispatcher should expect to find this train's

    A. leader lightly loaded with passengers
    B. leader heavily loaded with passengers
    C. follower more heavily loaded with passengers than usual
    D. follower more lightly loaded with passengers than usual

    11.____

12. If you, as an assistant train dispatcher, detect an error in an order issued to you by the train dispatcher, it is MOST important to

    A. point out the error to him
    B. try to carry out the order as issued
    C. put the order aside until the train dispatcher detects and corrects the order himself
    D. discuss it with another assistant train dispatcher

    12.____

13. Cars are scheduled for inspection based on information gathered from

    A. train register sheets   B. train interval sheets
    C. disposition sheets   D. mileage cards

    13.____

14. In tunnel areas where a *single track* operation must be performed without the signal protection of traffic control, a(n)

    A. *absolute block* must be maintained
    B. pilot must supervise the job

    14.____

C. assistant train dispatcher must supervise the job
D. wrong rail move is not allowed

15. The speed of a train that travels 6 miles in 12 minutes is _____ mph.   15._____

    A. 20   B. 30   C. 40   D. 50

Questions 16-20.

DIRECTIONS: Questions 16 through 20 apply to lever-type interlocking machines.

16. Spare levers should be painted   16._____

    A. white   B. blue   C. red   D. yellow

17. Switch levers should be painted   17._____

    A. red   B. blue   C. amber   D. black

18. Traffic levers should be painted   18._____

    A. blue   B. white   C. green   D. red

19. The various moves that can be made on an interlocking machine and the combination of   19._____
levers to be used for each of these moves is indicated on a

    A. manipulation chart   B. panel board
    C. disposition sheet   D. sequence chart

20. When the signal lever is in the reverse position and the signal indication light is dark, it   20._____
means that the

    A. call-on aspect is being displayed
    B. associated wayside signal is red
    C. associated wayside signal is clear
    D. emergency screw release should be used

Questions 21-25.

DIRECTIONS: Questions 21 through 25 apply to the pushbutton type of control panel (NX
and UR).

21. When no route has been set up and the home signal is at danger, the signal indication   21._____
light should be

    A. yellow   B. flashing yellow
    C. flashing red   D. dark

22. When a switch is in transit, the area of the control panel showing the switches should   22._____
flash

    A. red   B. white   C. green   D. blue

23. After a route has been properly established, the home signal clears. When this home sig-   23._____
nal clears, the signal indication light should change to a _____ color.

    A. green   B. yellow   C. red   D. white

24. A towerman cancels a route by _____ the proper entrance and exit _____.
    A. pulling; buttons
    B. pushing; buttons
    C. turning; buttons clockwise
    D. turning; buttons counterclockwise

24.____

25. When a switch is electrically locked, the area of the control panel showing the switch should flash

    A. white   B. amber   C. blue   D. yellow

25.____

KEY (CORRECT ANSWERS)

1.	A	11.	C
2.	C	12.	A
3.	C	13.	D
4.	B	14.	A
5.	D	15.	B
6.	A	16.	D
7.	D	17.	D
8.	C	18.	A
9.	B	19.	A
10.	C	20.	C

21.	D
22.	A
23.	B
24.	A
25.	A

TEST 3

1. How many additional cars are required to increase the present eight-car service to ten-car service, if the running time from terminal to terminal is 40 minutes, the relay time is 5 minutes at each end, and the headway is 10 minutes?   1.____

   A. 16   B. 18   C. 20   D. 22

2. Rapid transportation department bulletin boards are used for the posting of   2.____

   A. train schedules
   B. reports of employee accidents
   C. flexible schedules
   D. employees' daily work assignments

3. On the train-to-wayside radio system, the transceiver equipment mounted in the trains is called the   3.____

   A. relay station   B. base station
   C. cab unit   D. mobile unit

4. On the train-to-wayside radio system, the term command center refers to the   4.____

   A. base station
   B. train dispatcher's office
   C. desk trainmaster's office
   D. radio dispatcher's console

5. A light train that is being moved from one yard to another is called a   5.____

   A. drag   B. gap train
   C. extra train   D. pick up

6. When a car is moved from a particular track onto a main line track and returned to the adjacent track, the move is called a   6.____

   A. stretch   B. reroute   C. relay   D. drop back

7. Cars that are used to provide power for moving inoperative cars are called   7.____

   A. revenue cars   B. power cars
   C. extra cars   D. work motors

8. A section of track on which a train is NOT permitted to enter while it is occupied by another train is called a(n)   8.____

   A. pocket   B. absolute block
   C. gap   D. siding

9. Of the following items, the one that is usually NOT found at a blue light location is a(n)   9.____

   A. emergency exit   B. emergency alarm
   C. emergency telephone   D. fire extinguisher

10. According to the latest standard flagging instructions, a flagman should place his red lamp a MINIMUM distance of _____ feet from the work area.

    A. 50   B. 75   C. 100   D. 500

10.____

Questions 11-16.

DIRECTIONS: Questions 11 through 16 are based on the system of signal indications that is used on Division B (BMT and IND) and most of Division A (IRT).

11. A starting signal for a train at a terminal has three _____ lights.

    A. amber   B. green   C. blue   D. red

11.____

12. The signal aspect which means *proceed on the main route and be prepared to stop at the next signal* is

    A. green over yellow   B. yellow over green
    C. yellow over yellow   D. red over red over yellow

12.____

13. A signal that displays EITHER two horizontal red lights or two horizontal lunar white lights is called a _____ signal.

    A. marker   B. dwarf
    C. train order   D. gap filler

13.____

14. The signal aspect which means *approach at the allowable speed and then proceed on the diverging route* is

    A. green over green with an illuminated D signal
    B. yellow over green
    C. green over yellow
    D. yellow over yellow with an illuminated S signal

14.____

15. A signal with a fixed aspect that always indicates *stop and stay* is called a(n) _____ signal.

    A. dwarf   B. marker   C. home   D. approach

15.____

16. The signal aspect which requires a slow train speed movement past the signal into the yard is

    A. yellow over yellow over yellow
    B. yellow over yellow over lunar white
    C. green over green over yellow
    D. red over red over yellow

16.____

17. A tower horn signal consisting of three short blasts means that the

    A. road car inspector should contact the tower
    B. signal maintainer should contact the tower
    C. trains in the interlocking limits should proceed
    D. train has run past or stopped short of the station platform

17.____

18. The tower horn signal consisting of two short blasts means that the 18._____

    A. road car inspector should contact the tower
    B. train has run past or stopped short of the station platform
    C. trains in the interlocking should come to an immediate stop
    D. trains in the interlocking should proceed

19. A train horn signal of one long and one short blast means that the 19._____

    A. train is passing caution lights
    B. train crew needs the transit police
    C. motorman is requesting the towerman for a route
    D. motorman is asking for a signal maintainer

20. According to the rules, if an assistant train dispatcher finds a diamond ring, he should 20._____

    A. turn it over to the transit police
    B. forward it to the lost property office by special messenger
    C. personally take it to the lost property office after his tour of duty
    D. send it to the most convenient location equipped with lost property bags

21. The information on the *record of crews* sheet is used for paying 21._____

    A. assistant train dispatchers
    B. motorman instructors
    C. train dispatchers
    D. towerman

22. The color of the pencil used for entering information on mileage cards for the AM tour of duty is 22._____

    A. black   B. red   C. blue   D. green

23. Of the following, the HIGHEST level supervisor responsible for employees in yard service is the 23._____

    A. yardmaster   B. trainmaster
    C. train dispatcher   D. motorman instructor

24. In order for a train to leave a terminal, the condition of its brakes must be such that 24._____

    A. no brakes are cut out
    B. the brakes are cut out on less than 1/4 of the cars
    C. the brakes are cut out on less than 1/3 of the cars
    D. the brakes are cut out on less than 1/2 of the cars

25. Assume that, as an assistant train dispatcher, you find that your relief frequently reports five to ten minutes late. 25._____
Of the following, the BEST course of action you should take in this situation is to

    A. arrange to go home early the next day
    B. say nothing to your relief but report the matter to the trainmaster
    C. warn your relief that you will report him if his lateness continues
    D. put in a claim for overtime for extra time

KEY (CORRECT ANSWERS)

1.	B		11.	A
2.	D		12.	B
3.	D		13.	C
4.	C		14.	D
5.	A		15.	B
6.	C		16.	A
7.	D		17.	A
8.	B		18.	D
9.	A		19.	D
10.	C		20.	B

21.	D
22.	B
23.	B
24.	A
25.	C

———

EXAMINATION SECTION
TEST 1

DIRECTIONS: Each question or incomplete statement is followed by several suggested answers or completions. Select the one that BEST answers the question or completes the statement. *PRINT THE LETTER OF THE CORRECT ANSWER IN THE SPACE AT THE RIGHT.*

1. With respect to train connections at express stops during non-rush hours, a train dispatcher MUST hold trains lor meets whenever   1.____

    A. the timetable shows an increase in headway
    B. the platforms become unusually crowded
    C. there has been a serious delay and trains are starting to come through
    D. he can do so without causing undue delay

2. When a conductor reports to the train dispatcher at a terminal that some main lights in certain cars of his train are not lighted, the train dispatcher should   2.____

    A. hold that train for shopping and substitute another
    B. order the cars having the defective lights locked, but continue the train in service
    C. report the condition and the car numbers to the desk trainmaster's office and the car inspector
    D. report the condition and the car numbers to the cars and shops department and follow their instructions

3. If a train dispatcher finds it necessary to pull the emergency alarm because of heavy arcing and smoke beneath a train stopped at his station, the NEXT move he is required by the rules to make is to notify the   3.____

    A. transit police department
    B. nearest fire station
    C. trainmaster's office
    D. car maintenance department

4. A train dispatcher who wishes to flag a motorman past the point at which he is stationed can do so by moving a white lantern in a   4.____

    A. horizontal circle   B. vertical circle
    C. horizontal line   D. vertical line

5. One line of the transit system on which 11-car trains are operated during rush hours is the   5.____

    A. Queens-8th Avenue Line of the IND Division
    B. Fourth Avenue (Astoria-95th St.) Line of the BMT Division
    C. Concourse-Coney Island Line of the IND Division
    D. Times Square-Flushing Line of the IRT Division

6. When the two sets of amber lights which are located above the edge of the platform at each gap station are lighted, they usually signify that the   6.____

    A. motorman should release his brakes and start if he has the indication in his cab
    B. conductor should close the doors promptly so the train can start

    C.   conductor should keep the doors open until the lights go out
    D.   motorman should keep his brakes applied until the lights go out

7.   With respect to a color-light repeater signal in the subway, it is TRUE that such a signal   7._____

    A.   has fewer aspects than the signal it repeats
    B.   is located on the left-hand side of the track
    C.   cannot be seen until the main signal is reached
    D.   is always red until the train reaches it

8.   Of the following, the one which is NOT a fixed signal is a   8._____

    A.   yellow lantern hung on a column
    B.   resume speed sign mounted on the wall
    C.   train starting light
    D.   station car-stop marker

9.   A yellow aspect displayed by an automatic signal means   9._____

    A.   proceed prepared to stop within range of vision
    B.   proceed with caution prepared to stop at next signal
    C.   proceed at 10 M.P.H.
    D.   stop and then proceed with caution

10.   Because timetables for each station covering the period frrom 10:00 P.M. to 6:00 A.M.   10._____
have been issued to the public, conductors have been instructed to be especially careful
in regulating their trains to precisely the prescribed leaving times during this period. A
conductor can accomplish this regulation by

    A.   holding the doors open at each station until the time scheduled to leave
    B.   using appropriate bell or buzzer signals to contact the motorman
    C.   operating doors promptly to keep station stop time to a minimum
    D.   checking his watch against other clocks at every opportunity

11.   A recent General Order reads, in part, *IND Division Rail Car #103, temporarily assigned*   11._____
to the BMT Division, is equipped with trip on each end of car and may be operated on
open end of train.
This means that Car #103

    A.   has a cab from which the motorman can operate the train
    B.   should be placed between motor cars so as not to be tripped
    C.   can properly be the first car of a train although it is a trailer car
    D.   can safely be used as the last car when going against the current of traffic

12.   It is sometimes necessary to transfer cars from the Corona Shop located on the IRT Divi-   12._____
sion Queens Line to the Coney Island Shop of the BMT Division. The name of the station
near which trains can be transferred from the IRT Division to the BMT Division is

    A.   Ditmar's Blvd., Astoria
    B.   Queens Plaza
    C.   Roosevelt Ave., Jackson Heights
    D.   Willet's Point Blvd.

13. Two yellow markers are NOT used on the front end of _____ trains.   13._____

    A. extra   B. collection
    C. work   D. light

14. A train dispatcher noticed an express train pulling out of the station with a side door   14._____
open, and he pulled the emergency alarm which happened to be located just outside his
office. The train was some distance out of the station by that time, but the train dispatcher
could hear that the brake was being applied. He should then have

    A. telephoned the signal maintainer to relay the information about the open door to
the train crew
    B. taken his flagging lanterns and proceeded down the track to inform the crew about
the open door
    C. telephoned the trainmaster's office to report the incident
    D. telephoned the towerman at the next interlocking plant to place the signals on that
track at STOP

15. There is NO rapid transit tunnel under the East River at _____ Street.   15._____

    A. 60th   B. 53rd   C. 23rd   D. 14th

16. If the scheduled headway leaving a particular terminal is 5 minutes from 8:00 A.M. to   16._____
9:00 A.M., and the 8:25 interval must be removed from service without making a substi-
tution, the BEST adjustment of the adjacent intervals, assuming there is sufficient
advance notice, is to dispatch the 8:20 two minutes _____ and the 8:30 two minutes
_____ .

    A. late; early   B. late; late
    C. early; early   D. early; late

17. The locked *Lost Property* bags which are located at certain designated points on the   17._____
transit system are picked up by

    A. station supervisors   B. collecting agents
    C. special inspectors   D. railroad watchmen

18. An order states that train crews must not be ordered to skip any stops unless *an adjust-*   18._____
ment of the interval at the next gap point is not possible. This order clearly applies to

    A. a train which has been delayed
    B. a train which is ahead of schedule
    C. the leader of a train which has been delayed
    D. the follower of a train which is ahead of schedule

19. One line of the transit system which is NOT a four-track line is the _____ Line.   19._____

    A. IND-Concourse
    B. IRT-Lexington
    C. BMT-Fourth Avenue (Brooklyn)
    D. IND-Queens

20. A notice reads, in part, *When shop transfers are made up in yards for operation over the main line, there must be enough live motors coupled together to equal at least the number of oars to be pushed or pulled.* Using the symbol M for a motor car and T for a car to be pushed or pulled, a properly made up shop transfer in accordance with the notice would be   20.____

    A. T-T-M-M-M-T-T-M   B. M-T-T-M-M-T-T-M
    C. M-M-M-M-T-T-T-T   D. T-M-M-T-T-M-M-T

21. An illuminated model board in a conventional signal tower shows the   21.____

    A. lengths and destinations of approaching trains
    B. general arrangement of signals and switches in the vicinity
    C. aspects of the controlled signals of the interlocking
    D. routes that have been lined up by the towerman

22. The rapid transit station NEAREST the General Post Office in New York is   22.____

    A. 34th Street on the IND 8th Ave. Line
    B. Grand Central on the IRT Lexington Ave. Line
    C. Atlantic Ave. on the BMT Brighton Line
    D. Chambers St. on the BMT Nassau St. Loop

23. During non-rush hours, a train dispatcher at a time point is speaking on the public address system as the doors are opened on a train which has just come to a stop. He need NOT announce the   23.____

    A. name of the station
    B. destination of the train
    C. connections that can be made to other lines
    D. destination of the following train

24. Several months ago, the rush hour headway on the Rockaway Line was increased from 16 minutes to 24 minutes. This represents a reduction in train service of APPROXIMATELY   24.____

    A. 25%   B. 33%   C. 50%   D. 67%

Questions 25-32.

DIRECTIONS: Questions 25 through 32 refer to the portion of the Record of Traffic Count and the notes given below. Refer to this material when answering these items.

RECORD OF TRAFFIC COUNT

LINE: T2

STATION: CROSSROADS   TRACK: S.B. EXPRESS

Date: April 24

Head Car No.	Time	No. of Pass. in 3rd Car		Total Cars
		Arr.	Lv.	
6410	830	190	120	10
5704	833	190	120	10
6683	836	200	120	10
5996	839	210	130	10
1803	842	210	120	10
499	845	230	120	10
6341	848	230	110	10
887	851	240	100	10
6014	854	250	100	10
512	857	250	80	10

NOTE: 1. Crossroads Station is in midtown, and is a heavily used transfer point.
        2. Past traffic counts taken at Crossroads Station show that the distribution of passengers in the various cars of the train is approximately as follows:

POSITION OF CAR IN TRAIN	1	2	3	4	5	6	7	8	9	10
Arriving car load in percent of most heavily loaded arriving car	60	80	100	100	100	100	90	90	80	70
Leaving car load in percent of most heavily loaded leaving car	70	100	100	80	60	50	80	100	100	100

25. The number of passengers in the first car of the first train shown in the tabulation when it arrived in Crossroads Station was about   25._____

   A. 133   B. 126   C. 114   D. 108

26. The number of passengers in the last car of the 851 interval when it left Crossroads Station was about   26._____

   A. 190   B. 120   C. 100   D. 80

27. The total number of passengers on all ten cars of the 836 interval when it arrived at Crossroads Station was about   27._____

   A. 2000   B. 1740   C. 1620   D. 1400

28. The total number of passengers on all ten cars of the 830 interval when it left Crossroads Station was about   28._____

   A. 1400   B. 1080   C. 1044   D. 1008

29. Considering that Crossroads Station is a heavily used transfer point, the total number of passengers alighting from the 3rd cars of all of the ten trains shown MOST probably was   29.____

    A. 980   B. between 980 and 1080
    C. 1080   D. more than 1080

30. The total number of passengers by which the arriving load on all ten cars of the 845 interval exceeded the leaving load on that interval was   30.____

    A. 2001   B. 1080   C. 1008   D. 993

31. Of the following conclusions that may be drawn from examination of the car numbers in the first column, the one MOST likely to be correct is that   31.____

    A. at least 6000 cars are assigned to this service
    B. alternate trains have different destinations
    C. any car can be coupled in a train with any other car
    D. more than one type of car equipment is in use

32. From examination of the number of passengers arriving and leaving on successive trains, it is PROBABLY valid to conclude that   32.____

    A. many of the passengers exiting at Crossroads Station must report to work by 9:00 A.M.
    B. most people using line T2 southbound get off at or before Crossroads Station
    C. people riding past Crossroads Station generally report to work later than 9:00 A.M.
    D. line T2 is operating at practically its maximum capacity

33. With respect to entering upon and crossing the tracks in the subway, it is PROBABLY correct to say of a train dispatcher stationed at an intermediate time-point that such action is   33.____

    A. inexcusable at any time
    B. likely to be required very seldom
    C. probably required whenever there is a train delay
    D. probably required whenever it is necessary to transmit messages to train crews

34. When a N.Y.C.T.A. first aid kit is opened, it is NOT necessary to report the   34.____

    A. name of the person for whom the kit was opened
    B. kind of injury involved
    C. amount of each material used
    D. last previous date on which the kit was opened

35. An 0 displayed on the heat and ventilation board at a terminal during the winter season is an indication to crews that NO   35.____

    A. heat is to be turned on
    B. change is to be made in heating or ventilation
    C. windows are to be opened
    D. ventilators are to be closed

36. A ten-car train took 6 minutes to travel between two stations which are 3 miles apart. The average speed of the train was _____ M.P.H.   36.____

    A. 20   B. 25   C. 30   D. 35

37. The latest cars on the transit system are equipped with roller bearings which allow these cars to roll more easily than cars not so equipped. From the standpoint of operating personnel, the MOST important of the following consequences of rolling more easily is that the

    A. new trains are less noisy when rounding curves
    B. train crews must be alert to prevent rolling at certain station stops
    C. new trains can reach much higher speeds than older trains
    D. train crews are relieved of having to report hot bearings

37.____

38. In certain cases of single-track operation, a motorman is designated as *pilot* and no train may be admitted to the single-track without this designated *pilot* on board. Under this arrangement, it is clear that

    A. short trains must be run to avoid fatiguing the *pilot*
    B. flagmen are not needed
    C. regular train schedules are necessarily maintained without change
    D. two trains will not ordinarily follow one another in the same direction

38.____

39. The one of the following which is a train speed restriction in full accord with the rules and regulations is that a train is restricted to a maximum speed of

    A. 35 M.P.H. when skipping a station
    B. 25 M.P.H. when in an under-river tube
    C. 15 M.P.H. when entering a terminal
    D. 10 M.P.H. when not carrying passengers

39.____

40. A recent order requires that when motormen are operating trains in yards or other restricted areas they must operate from a standing position in the cab. The MOST probable reason for this requirement is that the standing position makes it easier for the motorman to

    A. read hand signals from the tower
    B. manipulate the train controls
    C. read dwarf signal indications
    D. see persons close to the trainway

40.____

41. The order in which employees in a particular title are scheduled to make their picks of tours of duty is determined PRIMARILY by each employee's

    A. last name, the names being arranged in alphabetical order
    B. length of service in the particular title
    C. attendance and service rating credit
    D. total length of service in the transit system

41.____

42. If a train dispatcher hears a long-short-long-short whistle signal from a train which is entering the station, the BEST of the following moves for him to make is to

    A. notify the signal maintainer
    B. send a platformman to see the motorman
    C. notify the trainmaster
    D. pull the emergency alarm

42.____

43. One entry that a train dispatcher is NOT required to make on a train register sheet is the   43.____

    A. name of the dispatcher
    B. reason for a late arrival
    C. name of the yard motorman on a put-in train
    D. name of the conductor on a regular passenger train

44. Certain lost articles turned in at terminals are required to be forwarded to the office by special messenger as soon as possible after being turned in. One such lost article would be a   44.____

    A. wallet containing considerable money
    B. loaded pistol
    C. hamper of fish
    D. press-type camera loaded with film

45. When a call-on signal in the subway is illuminated, the colors displayed on the home signal above the call-on are   45.____

    A. green over red   B. yellow over yellow
    C. red over yellow   D. red over red

46. An A.V.A. day may be accumulated by an hourly-rated employee as a consequence of being required to work   46.____

    A. four hours immediately following his regular tour
    B. on both Saturday and Sunday of the same weekend
    C. on a paid holiday
    D. on his regular day off

47. Because of changes in car construction, 9-car trains of the newest type are being operated on certain lines of the IRT Division where 10-car trains of the older type are still in operation. By logical reasoning, the change that is MOST probably the cause of running the shorter trains of new cars is the   47.____

    A. use of fluorescent instead of incandescent lighting
    B. addition of destination signs on the front and rear
    C. rearrangement of the side doors
    D. introduction of higher accelerating and braking rates

48. In addition to having supervision over assistant train dispatchers, the train dispatcher at a terminal has supervision over   48.____

    A. yard motormen, conductors, and car maintainers
    B. platformmen, assistant motorman instructions, and signal maintainers
    C. conductors in train service, platformmen, and road motormen
    D. road motormen, yard motormen, and signal maintainers

49. If a train that is carrying considerably less than a normal load is followed by one carrying considerably more than a normal load for the time of day and line involved, it is MOST likely that   49.____

    A. the first train is ahead of schedule and the second is on time
    B. the first train is on time and the second is behind schedule

C. both trains are ahead of schedule
D. both trains are behind schedule

50. When necessary to give a hand signal permitting a train to pass an interlocking signal indicating STOP, such hand signal must NOT be given until the   50._____

A. trainmaster has given his O.K.
B. train has come to a stop
C. motorman blows two blasts of the train whistle
D. train ahead has cleared the interlocking

_____

KEY (CORRECT ANSWERS)

1.	D	11.	C	21.	B	31.	D	41.	B
2.	C	12.	B	22.	A	32.	A	42.	B
3.	C	13.	A	23.	D	33.	B	43.	A
4.	D	14.	C	24.	B	34.	D	44.	A
5.	A	15.	C	25.	C	35.	A	45.	D
6.	C	16.	A	26.	C	36.	C	46.	C
7.	B	17.	B	27.	B	37.	B	47.	C
8.	A	18.	A	28.	D	38.	D	48.	C
9.	B	19.	A	29.	D	39.	C	49.	A
10.	A	20.	C	30.	D	40.	D	50.	B

_____

TEST 2

DIRECTIONS: Each question or incomplete statement is followed by several suggested answers or completions. Select the one that BEST answers the question or completes the statement. *PRINT THE LETTER OF THE CORRECT ANSWER IN THE SPACE AT THE RIGHT.*

1. The GREATEST number of passengers would probably be inconvenienced if, as a result of having the wrong marker lights displayed on the front end of a train,   1.____

   A. some passengers boarded the wrong train
   B. a towerman lined up and the motorman accepted the wrong route
   C. a platformman announced the wrong destination
   D. a flagman held up the train unnecessarily

2. Assume that you are a witness to an accident in the subway and that a stranger starts to question you about it.   2.____
   According to the rules, your proper action is to

   A. ask him for his credentials
   B. refer him to the transit authority legal department
   C. answer only those questions about which you have firsthand information
   D. telephone the trainmaster's office and request instructions

3. An assistant train dispatcher suspects that the man who is to relieve him is under the influence of liquor. In this case, the assistant dispatcher should   3.____

   A. refuse relief and continue on duty without taking any other action
   B. accept relief and ignore the situation, since it is no longer his responsibility
   C. accept relief but stay around awhile to see if the reliever can work properly
   D. refuse relief and report his suspicion to the dispatcher or trainmaster

4. At a subway station located in the financial district of Manhattan, an assistant train dispatcher could normally expect the GREATEST concentration of passenger traffic to occur during the weekday hour between   4.____

   A. 4:30 P.M. and 5:30 P.M.   B. 5:30 P.M. and 6:30 P.M.
   C. 7:00 A.M. and 8:00 A.M.   D. 9:00 A.M. and 10:00 A.M.

5. A subway passenger CANNOT go directly (without changing trains) from   5.____

   A. Manhattan to Brooklyn   B. Queens to Brooklyn
   C. Queens to The Bronx   D. Brooklyn to The Bronx

6. A rule of the subway system is that the transit police department MUST be notified first whenever an ambulance is needed. A logical reason for this rule is to   6.____

   A. help in apprehending legal offenders
   B. enable the transit police to check the need for an ambulance
   C. prevent duplication of calls
   D. prevent unnecessary ambulance calls

7. When an unusual situation arises, and you cannot contact your immediate supervisor to check the method of handling the situation, it would be BEST for you to   7.____

A. ask some of the experienced motormen at your terminal for their advice
B. telephone to another assistant dispatcher for advice
C. telephone the trainmaster's office for instructions
D. take no action until your superior returns

Questions 8-16.

DIRECTIONS: Questions 8 through 16 are based on the paragraph below. Refer to this paragraph when answering these questions.

At about 3 o'clock on a weekday afternoon, a southbound passenger express train came to a stop at a red automatic signal midway between stations. After about three minutes, conductor Johnson came forward and asked motorman Smith why the train was stopped and how long it would stay, because it was his (the conductor's) duty according to rules to notify the passengers. Smith did not know the reason and together with Johnson decided to call up the trainmaster's office to find out the facts. They walked to the nearest blue light, Smith taking his reverser key and brake handle with him. When they reached the blue light location, Smith pulled the operating handle of the emergency alarm box to remove power from the third rail as insurance that no unauthorized person could start the train in his absence; Johnson then used the telephone to call the trainmaster's office. Johnson found out that the train ahead had a grounded master controller in the operating can and that as soon as power was restored to the third rail Smith would have to pull up to the train ahead and transfer its passengers to his train. This was done, and the disabled train was ordered out of service while Johnson's train continued in regular passenger service. The delay to Johnson's train at the scene was 15 minutes. After they arrived at their home terminal (the north terminal of the line), Smith and Johnson made written reports of the incident.

8.   The MOST serious error or infraction of the rules committed by Johnson was   8.____

A. leaving the train unattended
B. failing to wait four minutes before going forward
C. not notifying the passengers
D. waiting as long as three minutes before going forward

9.   One of Smith's actions which was ENTIRELY correct was   9.____

A. pulling the emergency alarm
B. having Johnson accompany him
C. taking the reverser key and brake handle along when he got off the train
D. leaving his train at the signal instead of pulling up to the blue light

10.   In making out written reports when they reached their home terminal, Smith and Johnson   10.____

A. acted in accordance with the rules and regulations of the N.Y.C.T.A.
B. did unnecessary extra work because they had already reported the incident to the trainmaster by telephone
C. waited too long; they should have made written reports at the first gap station
D. went beyond the rules; the delay was only 15 minutes which does not require any reports

11. The trainmaster overlooked the opportunity to stress a safety precaution in that he   11.____

    A. allowed Smith's train to pull up to the train ahead
    B. permitted the passengers to walk from the disabled train to the following one
    C. had the train with the grounded master controller taken out of service
    D. failed to remind Johnson to open the conductor's valve on the train ahead while the passengers were transferring

12. In order for Smith to be able to pass the red signal and close in on the train ahead, he MUST have first   12.____

    A. telephoned the nearby tower and had the towerman clear the signal
    B. whistled for the signal maintainer to tie down the automatic stop
    C. keyed-by the signal as prescribed in the book of rules
    D. telephoned the section dispatcher to send a flagman to flag him by

13. Before leaving his train to make the telephone call, the motorman should have   13.____

    A. sounded the appropriate whistle signal
    B. set up one or more hand brakes
    C. opened the conductor's valve on the head end
    D. cut in the car emergency lights

14. Pulling of the emergency alarm by Smith showed   14.____

    A. quick thinking; he probably saved the train ahead from further damage
    B. lack of thought; there was no trouble in his area to warrant such action
    C. knowledge of the rules; such action is required in similar situations
    D. consideration for passenger safety; this action probably avoided panic

15. The aspect of the signal at which Smith stopped his train was PROBABLY   15.____

    A. two red lights above a yellow light
    B. two red lights, one above the other
    C. a single red light
    D. two red lights, side by side

16. The amount of delay to Smith and Johnson in returning to their home terminal   16.____

    A. must have been exactly 15 minutes
    B. depended mainly on the scheduled running time between terminals
    C. may have been more or less than 15 minutes
    D. depended on how quickly a replacement for the train taken out of service was obtained

17. One positive way in which a single-light interlocking color-light signal can be distinguished from an automatic color-light signal is by observing the   17.____

    A. differences in colors displayed
    B. inscription on the number plate
    C. shape of the lenses
    D. signal mounting

18. As part of his regular duties, an assistant train dispatcher may be required to   18.____

    A. instruct newly appointed towermen in his section
    B. keep a gap sheet at a specified location
    C. make certain tests of trains at his terminal
    D. take charge of a yard

19. If an assistant train dispatcher located in an interlocking tower wants to contact the signal   19.____
maintainer, the tower horn signal to be sounded is _____ blast(s).

    A. two long and one short   B. one long and one short
    C. three short   D. two short and one long

20. The terminal which is NOT elevated is _____ Line.   20.____

    A. Far Rockaway on the Rockaway
    B. Stillwell Avenue on the Coney Island
    C. Van Cortlandt Park on the Broadway-7th Avenue
    D. 207th Street on the Washington Heights

21. If an emergency alarm box located on a four-track section of the subway is pulled, it will   21.____
cause third rail power to be removed from

    A. the one track nearest the box only
    B. both local tracks only
    C. both express tracks only
    D. all four tracks

22. The gauge of rail is the distance between the   22.____

    A. inside edges of the running rails
    B. outside edges of the running rails
    C. centers of the third rail and the near running rail
    D. centers of the third rail and the far running rail

23. The service on a certain four-track line consists of 20 trains per hour on each express   23.____
track and 16 trains per hour on each local track. The total number of all trains passing a
given point on this line in any 10-minute period is

    A. 6   B. 9   C. 12   D. 15

24. If the distance between two signals on the transit system is 750 feet and one signal is at   24.____
stationing 1275 + 20, the other could be stationing

    A. 525 + 20   B. 1200 + 70   C. 1282 + 70   D. 2025 + 20

25. If a passenger train arrives at a time point ahead of time, the assistant train dispatcher   25.____
could expect to find this train's

    A. follower heavily loaded   B. follower lightly loaded
    C. leader heavily loaded   D. leader lightly loaded

26. On a run between two express stops, an express train passes four local stations. If the average time required for a local train to brake, make a station stop, and accelerate back to normal speed is 45 seconds for each station, then the time that can be saved by going express rather than local between these two express stops is NEAREST to _____ minute(s).

26.____

    A. one   B. two   C. three   D. four

Questions 27-41.

DIRECTIONS: Questions 27 through 41 are based on the station layout and portion of a gap sheet for station C shown below and on the following page. Refer to this material when answering these questions. Station C is a time point on the Lake Line, which has no branch lines. Operations proceed without delays unless otherwise stated in a question.

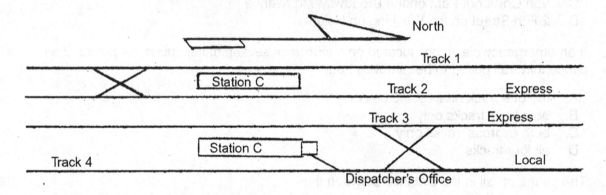

GAP SHEET - STATION C - DAILY

SOUTHBOUND			NORTHBOUND		
RUN NO.	LV LOCAL	LV EXPRESS	RUN NO.	LV LOCAL	LV EXPRESS
10	1010		11	1011	
12		1010	13		1012
14	1015		15	1017	
16		1016	17		1018
18	1020		19	1023	
20		1022	21		1024
22	1026		23	1030	
24		1028	25		1032
26	1032		27	1040	
28		1034	29		1040
11	1040		10	1050	
32		1040	31		1050
19	1050		18	1100	
34		1050	33		1100
23	1100		26	1112	
13		1100	12		1112
27	1110		11	1124	
21		1110	20		1124
10	1120		19	1136	
25		1120	28		1136
18	1130		22	1148	
29		1130	32		1148
31		1140	10	1200	
15	1142		24		1200
33		1150	18	1212	
11	1154		21		1212
12		1202	15	1224	
19	1206		25		1224
20		1214	11	1236	
22	1218	1226	29		1236
28			19	1248	
10	1230		31		1248
32		1238	22	100	
18	1242		33		100
24		1250	10	110	
15	1254		12		112
21		102	18	120	
11	106		20		124
25		114	35	130	
19	116		28		136
29		126	15	140	
36	126		32		146
			11	150	
			24		156

27. One crew which evidently clears after arrival at the south local terminal is the crew on run number   27.____

    A. 10   B. 14   C. 18   D. 22

28. One crew which evidently clears after arrival at the north express terminal is the crew on run number   28.____

    A. 13   B. 17   C. 21   D. 25

29. Assuming that crews are allowed five minutes between arrival and leaving at each terminal, the terminal-to-terminal running time for express run number 29 on the trip leaving station C at 1040 is   29.____

    A. 1 hr. 56 min.   B. 1 hr. 46 min.
    C. 58 min.   D. 53 min.

30. The scheduled round trip time for local run number 10 leaving station C northbound at 1050 is _____ minutes.   30.____

    A. 70   B. 60   C. 50   D. 40

31. Assuming a five minute relay at the terminal, the running time from station C to the north terminal for run number 18 on the trip leaving station C at 1100 is _____ minutes.   31.____

    A. 12 1/2   B. 15   C. 25   D. 30

32. Run numbers 13 and 23 southbound are *meets* at 1100. If run number 23 is one minute late, the proper action to take is to   32.____

    A.   hold run numbers 13 and 21 one-half minute each
    B.   let the express leave on time without a meet
    C.   hold run number 13 for one minute
    D.   hole run number 21 for the meet

33. If run number 20 southbound scheduled to leave at 1022 arrives one minute early, the assistant train dispatcher should   33.____

    A.   hold run number 18 for one minute to make a *meet*
    B.   merely hold the train until 1022
    C.   ask the preceding time point if the train left early
    D.   check whether the schedule time can be cut by one minute

34. Two locals and two expresses are scheduled to be rung off at exactly the same time at   34.____

    A. 1120   B. 1112   C. 1110   D. 1100

35. The number of different motormen who stop at station C between 1035 and 1140, inclusive, is   35.____

    A. 25   B. 24   C. 21   D. 18

36. The total number of different crew tricks shown in the northbound local runs is   36.____

    A. 10   B. 12   C. 15   D. 22

37. The crew which has time for lunch at the north local terminal is on run number   37.____

    A. 11   B. 15   C. 19   D. 23

38. One tour which probably clears at the south express terminal is run number   38.____

    A. 24   B. 20   C. 16   D. 12

39. If all northbound local trains stopping at station C from 1020 to 1120, inclusive, have 8   39.____
    cars, the total number of cars on these trains is

    A. 48   B. 64   C. 96   D. 128

40. The terminal which is FARTHEST from station C is the destination of the   40.____

    A. northbound locals   B. northbound expresses
    C. southbound locals   D. southbound expresses

41. The total number of northbound locals scheduled to be at a ten-minute headway during   41.____
    the period shown is

    A. 3   B. 5   C. 7   D. 8

42. The transit system divisions that have stations at the New York Coliseum are the   42.____

    A. BMT and IRT   B. IND and BMT
    C. IRT and IND   D. IND, BMT, and IRT

43. A train is bound for the yard if both of its front marker lights are   43.____

    A. red   B. green   C. white   D. yellow

44. Block signals which are normally at danger and which enforce train operation at a prede-   44.____
    termined reduced speed are classified as _____ signals.

    A. G.T.   B. S.T.   C. approach   D. dwarf

45. Because the latest types of cars used in the subway have dynamic brakes,   45.____

    A. higher speeds are attained
    B. less steel dust is deposited
    C. weight of cars is reduced
    D. longer trains have become practical

46. The only rapid transit line which crosses the Harlem River on a bridge is the _____   46.____
    Line.

    A. Pelham Bay Park   B. Woodlawn
    C. Dyre Avenue   D. Van Cortlandt Park

47. The model board above a unit-lever interlocking machine indicates   47.____

    A. which tracks are occupied by trains
    B. the destinations of approaching trains
    C. which signals are clear
    D. which routes are set up

48. There is NO under-river subway tunnel from Manhattan at _____ Street.   48._____

   A.   Whitehall   B.   Fulton   C.   23rd   D.   42nd

49. When filling out a lost property form, an assistant dispatcher need NOT record   49._____

   A.   the name of the person turning in the article
   B.   a description of the article
   C.   an estimate of the value of the article
   D.   the place found or the time turned in

50. Bulletin orders are sometimes reissued without change and are marked as reissues of   50._____
previous orders. The purpose of this procedure is USUALLY to

   A.   replace worn-out orders on bulletin boards
   B.   remind employees that the order is still important
   C.   supersede prior conflicting bulletins
   D.   remind employees that supervision is alert and active

---

KEY (CORRECT ANSWERS)

1. B	11. D	21. D	31. A	41. D
2. B	12. C	22. A	32. C	42. C
3. D	13. B	23. C	33. B	43. D
4. A	14. B	24. C	34. D	44. A
5. C	15. C	25. A	35. D	45. B
6. C	16. C	26. C	36. A	46. D
7. C	17. B	27. B	37. B	47. A
8. A	18. B	28. B	38. C	48. C
9. C	19. B	29. D	39. A	49. C
10. A	20. D	30. A	40. D	50. B

TEST 3

DIRECTIONS: Each question or incomplete statement is followed by several suggested answers or completions. Select the one that BEST answers the question or completes the statement. *PRINT THE LETTER OF THE CORRECT ANSWER IN THE SPACE AT THE RIGHT.*

1. Rule 35(e) reads as follows: *Unless otherwise directed by proper authority, trains must be operated in accordance with the schedule.* The PROPER authority referred to in this rule is the

   A. chief schedule maker   B. road trainmaster
   C. desk trainmaster   D. motorman instructor

   1.____

2. A motorman operating a 10-car train of *R* cars with two conductors reports failure of the motorman's indication.
   He should be instructed to

   A. discharge passengers immediately and remove the train from service
   B. wait for the road car inspector and then proceed with the inspector on board
   C. continue with the train in service using buzzer signals after a clear understanding with the first position conductor
   D. wait for the road car inspector and have the indication repaired before proceeding

   2.____

3. There is NO East River bridge at _____ Street.

   A. 42nd   B. Delancey   C. 59th   D. Canal

   3.____

4. Car information is entered on Trips and Mileage *Data.* Sheets in different colored pencil by the midnight, A.M., and P.M. forces. The color which is required to be used for such purpose by the midnight forces is

   A. green   B. red   C. blue   D. black

   4.____

5. If a train dispatcher is required to work one hour in excess of his regularly scheduled hours on any day, he will receive for this work

   A. no extra pay or extra time off
   B. pay for one and one-half hours at his regular rate
   C. pay for one hour at his regular rate
   D. one hour off with pay

   5.____

6. A CORRECT statement according to the rules is that speed of trains

   A. is restricted to 15 M.P.H. over all diverging routes unless otherwise indicated
   B. on straight main-line tracks is restricted to 35 M.P.H.
   C. in under-river tubes between shafts is restricted to 15 M.P.H. when operating around sharp curves
   D. entering terminals unless otherwise restricted must not exceed 15 M.P.H.

   6.____

7. One of the prescribed duties of a train dispatcher is to

    A. supervise all employees in train and yard service in his section
    B. check the performance of train crews on the road
    C. authorize the making up of extra trains when necessary
    D. prepare timetables and crew sheets

7._____

8. An express train which has been diverted to the local track is required to stop

    A. at all stations if the schedule can be maintained
    B. at all stations regardless of whether the schedule can be maintained
    C. only at express stations unless otherwise directed
    D. only at the stations which are time points

8._____

9. Train dispatchers should be qualified to operate all interlocking towers in their sections. The statement which is NOT a reason for this requirement is that a dispatcher may have to

    A. operate any of these towers in an emergency
    B. supervise the towermen in his section
    C. answer questions of a relief towerman about a tower
    D. qualify new towermen in his section

9._____

10. If a series of automatic signals were to have the S.T. feature added, the purpose would PROBABLY be to

    A. compensate for changes in passenger loads
    B. make the signals lever-controlled
    C. make it possible to operate at a closer headway
    D. reduce the speed of trains

10._____

11. The proper standard symbol to use on a train register sheet to indicate that a certain car has been cut from a train at the terminal is to draw a _____ the car number.

    A. circle around   B. bracket at each end of
    C. straight line under   D. box around

11._____

Questions 12-22.

DIRECTIONS: Questions 12 through 22 are based on the portion of the Line M timetable and the motormen's work programs shown on the following page. Refer to this information in answering these questions. Line M is a two-track line without branch lines. Assume that operations proceed without delays unless otherwise noted. An X in any box indicates that an entry has been intentionally omitted because it can readily be determined from the data given.

TIMETABLE - LINE M - DAILY

Aide St.	Bass St.	Cape St.	Flint Ave.		Cape St.	Bass St.	Aide St.	
Lv.	Lv.	Lv.	Arr.	Lv.	Lv.	Lv.	Arr.	Lv.
816	826	839	850	854	905	918	928	936
822	832	845	856	900	911	924	934	942
828	838	851	902	906	917	930	940	X
834	844	857	908	912	923	936	946	954
924	934	947	958	1002	1013	1026	1036	1044
930	940	953	1004	1008	1019	1032	1042	1050
936	946	959	1010	1014	1025	1038	1048	1056
942	952	1005	1016	1020	1031	1044	1054	1102

MOTORMEN'S WORK PROGRAMS - LINE M - DAILY

Run No.	M/M	Report		Aide St.	Flint Ave.		Aide St.		Flint Ave.		Aide St.	Relieved		Time on Duty	
		Time	Place	Lv.	Arr.	Lv.	Arr.	Lv.	Arr.	Lv.	Arr.	Time	Place	Act.	Allow
137	Gard	149	Aide	204	238	243	317	328	402	407	441			X	800
				452	526	531	605	650	724	731	805				
				828	902	906	940					940	Aide	X	800
138	John	201	Aide	216	250	255	329	340	414	419	453				
				504	538	543	617	700	734	741	815				
				834	908	912	946					946	Aide	745	800
144	Lee	251	Aide	306	340	345	419	430	504	509	543				
				554	628	633	707	746	820	826	900				
				912	946	950	1024					1024	Aide	733	800
145	Nile	X	Aide	317	351	356	430	441	515	520	554				
				605	639	644	718	816	850	854	928				
				942	1016	1020	1054					1054	Aide	751	800

12. The number of round trips in Lee's tour of duty is

    A. 4   B. 5   C. 8   D. 10

12.____

13. The motorman whose tour gives him the MOST time for his lunch period is

    A. Gard   B. John   C. Lee   D. Nile

13.____

14. On a day when Lee is delayed by traffic conditions so that he clears twenty-seven minutes late, he is entitled, according to the Working Conditions, to be paid at his regular rate of pay for

    A. 8 hours
    B. 8 hours, 18 minutes
    C. 8 hours, 27 minutes
    D. 8 hours, 41 minutes

14.____

15. If Nile is delayed by traffic conditions so that he clears twenty-seven minutes late, he is entitled, according to the Working Conditions, to be paid at his regular rate of pay for

    A. 8 hours
    B. 8 hours, 18 minutes
    C. 8 hours, 27 minutes
    D. 8 hours, 41 minutes

15.____

16. Assuming no cuts or adds, the cars which leave Aide St. at 816 will later arrive at Flint at

    A. 854   B. 936   C. 1048   D. 1130

16.____

17. Because of an emergency, John was required to take out Gard's last trip from Aide St. To do this, John's relay time at Aide St. had to be cut to _____ minutes.

    A. 6   B. 13   C. 19   D. 23

17.____

18. Of the 14 intervals shown in the timetable leaving Aide St., the number covered by the four tours of duty shown in the work programs is

    A. 2   B. 3   C. 4   D. 5

18.____

19. The two motormen whose tours give them the MOST opportunities to speak to each other at Aide St. are

    A. Gard and John
    B. John and Lee
    C. Lee and Nile
    D. Nile and Gard

19.____

20. At 800, the dispatcher at Flint Ave. receives a telephone message for Lee, and promptly relays the message to the dispatcher at Aide St. Assuming no intermediate dispatching points, the EARLIEST that Lee can receive the message is

    A. 810   B. 815   C. 820   D. 825

20.____

21. Except for his reporting and lunch periods, the LONGEST time Lee has at Aide St. is _____ minutes.

    A. 10   B. 11   C. 12   D. 13

21.____

22. Gard's scheduled actual time on duty is _____ hrs., _____ min.

    A. 7; 17   B. 7; 45   C. 7; 51   D. 8; 0

22.____

23. When, due to an emergency or to failure of a motorman to report, it becomes necessary for a terminal dispatcher to fill a road trick with a member of his local force, first priority, according to latest instructions, MUST be given to the

    A. board motorman
    B. extra list men (no assignment)
    C. vacation relief man (no assignment)
    D. qualified switchman

23.____

24. Assume that the present timetable provides for 15 trains per hour on one track at a certain time point. If the timetable is changed to provide 24 trains per hour on this track, the average change in headway will be _____ minute(s).

    A. 1   B. 1 1/4   C. 1 1/2   D. 2 1/2

24.____

Questions 25-37.

DIRECTIONS: Questions 25 through 37 are based on the track layout and table of car service shown below. Consult this sketch and table in answering these questions.

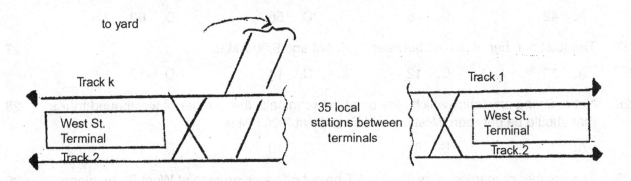

TRAIN SERVICE - WEST ST. TERMINAL - WEEKDAYS

ARRIVING				LEAVING			
From	To	Headway (Minutes)	No. Cars	From	To	Headway (Minutes)	No. Cars
12:25 AM	1:25 AM	10	6	12:03 AM	12:51 AM	12	6
1:36	3:00	12	6	1:06	4:36	15	4
3:15	6:45	15	4	4:48	5:48	10	6
6:57	7:57	10	6	5:56	6:28	8	8
8:05	8:37	8	8	6:33	8:58	5	10
8:42	11:07	5	10	9:05	9:40	7	10
1:14	11:49	7	10	9:47	2:06 PM	7	8
1:56	4:15 PM	7	8	2:11 PM	3:06	5	8
4:20 PM	5:15	5	8	3:11	5:11	5	10
5:20	7:20	5	10	5:18	6:00	7	10
7:27	8:09	7	10	6:07	6:56	7	8
8:16	9:05	7	8	7:06	10:06	10	8
9:15	12:15 AM	10	8	10:16	11:16	10	6
				11:27	11:51	12	6

NOTES:
1. The line between West St. and East St. is a 2-track line without any branch lines.
2. Two cars are cut off the 2:12 AM arrival at West St. and the remaining 4 cars dispatched to the road at 2:21 AM.
3. The relay time at East St. is 9 minutes for all trains.
4. Trains which remain in passenger service lay over at West St. for not less than 5 minutes nor more than twice the shorter headway (arriving or leaving) in effect at any particular time.
5. The scheduled terminal-to-terminal running time is exactly one hour.
6. All trains are made up of *married pairs*.
7. All operations proceed without delays unless otherwise stated.

25. The TOTAL number of trains in passenger service at 12:00 noon is   25.____

    A. 18   B. 20   C. 22   D. 24

26. The number of men needed to just crew all the trains in passenger service at 8:45 AM is   26.____

    A. 42   B. 48   C. 56   D. 60

27. The total number of put-ins between 5:00 AM and 9:00 AM is   27.____

    A. 10   B. 12   C. 14   D. 17

28. Not counting any trains which may be at the terminals, the number of westbound trains that should be between West St. and East St. at 2:00 PM is   28.____

    A. 8   B. 9   C. 10   D. 11

29. The number of *married pairs* that MUST be cut off trains arriving at West St. between 9:45 AM and 10:45 AM is   29.____

    A. 7   B. 9   C. 14   D. 18

30. The TOTAL number of cars that are adds (not including put-ins) from 3:00 PM to 5:30 PM is   30.____

    A. 22 or 24   B. 44 or 46   C. 68 or 70   D. 84 or 86

31. The time interval between the last A.M. put-in and the first A.M. lay-up is CLOSEST to _____ minutes.   31.____

    A. 15   B. 30   C. 45   D. 60

32. The average schedule time per station is NEAREST to _____ seconds.   32.____

    A. 94   B. 97   C. 100   D. 103

33. If the intermediate stations are uniformly spaced, then if a train is stopped in a station at the time of minimum headway, his follower should be _____ station behind.   33.____

    A. stopped at the 3rd
    B. in motion between the 3rd and 2nd
    C. stopped at the 2nd
    D. in motion between the 2nd and 1st

34. Cars are NOT added or cut, nor are trains put in, or laid up, at or about   34.____

    A. 1:00 AM   B. 7:00 AM   C. 1:00 PM   D. 7:00 PM

35. The TOTAL number of *married pairs* required to maintain the service on this line, allowing five percent for gap trains and shopping, is   35.____

    A. 135   B. 142   C. 270   D. 284

36. If the dispatcher at West St. is notified at 3:50 AM that the train scheduled to arrive at 4:00 AM will be 10 minutes late because of a temporary blockade, the dispatcher should   36.____

A. dispatch his gap train on time and lay up the delayed train on arrival
B. dispatch the delayed train and its leader 5 minutes late each
C. dispatch all trains on time
D. call the desk trainmaster for orders

37. The total number of scheduled eastbound intervals in a 24-hour period is   37._____

    A. 176   B. 187   C. 198   D. 209

38. If a special inspector identifies himself and asks for information about a particular motor-   38._____
man from the train dispatcher at a terminal, the dispatcher should, in every case,

    A. give the information and cooperate to the best of his knowledge
    B. request the special inspector to show written authorization
    C. refer his questions to the trainmaster
    D. refer the special inspector to the crew dispatcher

39. According to outstanding Instructions, the train dispatcher who observes an illuminated   39._____
smoke detector light must FIRST notify the

    A. trainmaster   B. telephone maintainer
    C. towerman   D. signal maintainer

40. The speed setting of a series of G.T. signals on a 1-mile stretch of track between succes-   40._____
sive express stops is changed from 30 M.P.H. to 35 M.P.H. The change in running time
as a result of this change in speed is NEAREST to _____ seconds.

    A. 7   B. 12   C. 17   D. 22

41. The running time between two local terminals is 40 minutes. If the average speed of the   41._____
trains on this run is 15 M.P.H., the distance between these terminals is APPROXI-
MATELY _____ miles.

    A. 8   B. 10   C. 12   D. 14

42. If a train dispatcher pulls an emergency alarm in the subway, it will cause the removal of   42._____
power from the third rails in the vicinity and also

    A. start the exhaust fans and sound an alarm in the trainmaster's office
    B. sound an alarm in the nearest fire house and turn on the emergency car lights
    C. sound an alarm in the trainmaster's office and cause all the signals in the area to
       go to danger
    D. start the exhaust fans and connect the adjacent telephone to the trainmaster's
       office

43. It is common knowledge among railroad men that a speed of 15 miles per hour is exactly   43._____
equal to 22 feet per second. In accordance with this rule, select the FASTEST of the following speeds:

    A. 70 feet per second   B. 50 miles per hour
    C. 0.9 mile per minute   D. 4500 feet per minute

44. A towerman calls the attention of the dispatcher to the fact that a certain section of track   44.____
    is occupied by the Sperry Rail Car, but that the model board does not indicate occupancy
    of the track section. The cause of this condition is MOST likely

    A. a broken rail
    B. the shortness of the track section
    C. an incorrect route set-up
    D. the lightness of the rail car

45. Route request buttons have been installed at certain home signals. These buttons are to   45.____
    be operated by the motorman when the home signal is at danger and no call-on is dis-
    played, or when an improper route is displayed. The PRINCIPAL advantage of such route
    request buttons over the use of the train whistle is that, with the buttons, the motorman

    A. need not come to a stop to request a route
    B. must come to a full stop to request a route
    C. is less likely to make an error
    D. is giving a more precise indication

46. The train on which you are riding takes 24 seconds to go from Signal M4-630 to M4-617   46.____
    (Signal 6304/M to Signal 6174/M in IRT nomenclature). The average speed of the train
    between these signals was MOST probably in the range from _____ M.P.H.

    A. 20 to 25   B. 25 to 30   C. 30 to 35   D. 35 to 40

47. A recent bulletin states, in part, that windows of unoccupied motormen's cabs must be   47.____
    kept closed at all times. The reason given in the bulletin for this requirement is that
    closed cab windows help to

    A. prevent vandalism
    B. keep the cab clean
    C. prevent use of the cab for immoral purposes
    D. keep the cab dry

48. When a certain job on a track is finished and the flagging protection is removed, the color   48.____
    of the lamp or flag to be removed last is

    A. white   B. yellow   C. green   D. red

49. On a portion of track where one-block-overlap automatic signals are used, the indica-   49.____
    tions of the three signals immediately behind a train, starting with the one NEAREST the
    train, are

    A. red, yellow, yellow   B. red, red, red
    C. red, yellow, green   D. red, red, yellow

50. Certain service cars must never be placed on the open end of a train. Based on your   50.____
    knowledge of service car equipment, you should know that this restriction applies to ser-
    vice cars which are NOT equipped with

    A. marker lights   B. hand brakes
    C. automatic couplers   D. trip cocks

KEY (CORRECT ANSWERS)

1.	C	11.	B	21.	C	31.	B	41.	B
2.	A	12.	B	22.	C	32.	C	42.	A
3.	A	13.	D	23.	B	33.	A	43.	C
4.	D	14.	A	24.	C	34.	C	44.	D
5.	D	15.	B	25.	B	35.	B	45.	D
6.	D	16.	D	26.	C	36.	C	46.	D
7.	A	17.	B	27.	D	37.	B	47.	A
8.	C	18.	C	28.	B	38.	A	48.	C
9.	D	19.	A	29.	B	39.	D	49.	D
10.	C	20.	C	30.	B	40.	C	50.	D

EXAMINATION SECTION
TEST 1

DIRECTIONS: Each question or incomplete statement is followed by several suggested answers or completions. Select the one that BEST answers the question or completes the statement. *PRINT THE LETTER OF THE CORRECT ANSWER IN THE SPACE AT THE RIGHT.*

1.   S.T. signals are used PRIMARILY to   1.____

    A.   permit a train to come close to its leader at a station
    B.   enforce operation at a predetermined reduced speed at all times
    C.   indicate when it is safe for a train to cross over to another track
    D.   control train movements between shop and yard storage tracks

2.   A train does not start when the train dispatcher gives the starting signal, but the motor-   2.____
man blows four short whistle blasts and, after a pause, four more. It would be BEST for
the train dispatcher to promptly

    A.   notify the trainmaster's office
    B.   put in a call for the signal maintainer
    C.   try to locate the car inspector
    D.   check with the towerman

3.   The main transit authority Lost and Found Office is NEAREST to the   3.____

    A.   Battery Tunnel   B.   Manhattan Bridge
    C.   Williamsburgh Bridge   D.   Belt Parkway

4.   Motormen have been instructed to leave all whistle cut-out cocks in cabs open unless the   4.____
whistle has failed, in which case they must promptly report the failure. The LOGICAL reason for leaving the whistle cut-out cocks open is to

    A.   insure that the whistle will be used
    B.   have the whistle ready to operate whenever necessary
    C.   establish a uniform procedure to simplify car inspection
    D.   encourage motormen to test the whistles each trip

5.   On the latest type of interlocking control machine in use on the transit system, a route   5.____
which is completely lined up is indicated by a

    A.   continuous line of white light
    B.   series of white *bulls eyes*
    C.   continuous line of red light
    D.   continuous line of brass strips

Questions 6-29.

DIRECTIONS: Questions 6 through 29 are based on the sketch and the portion of a train register sheet for Upper Road shown at the end of this test. Refer to this material
when answering these questions. Assume that operations proceed without
delays unless otherwise specified in a particular question.

6. The total number of inspection cars shown on the head end of road trains leaving Upper Road is

    A. 0   B. 2   C. 10   D. 18

6.____

7. The total number of yard motormen making the adds, cuts, put-ins, and lay-ups during the time covered by the train register

    A. was 2
    B. was 3
    C. was 5
    D. cannot be determined from the information given

7.____

8. It is clear that, when motorman Brun took ten cars to the yard shortly after 8:30, the train did NOT include car number

    A. 123   B. 47   C. 78   D. 189

8.____

9. The total number of trains shown arriving late is

    A. 2   B. 3   C. 4   D. 5

9.____

10. The scheduled layover at Upper Road for the train scheduled to arrive at 8:00 was _____ minutes.

    A. 3   B. 6   C. 9   D. 12

10.____

11. From the time of departure for the road of the first put-in train shown to the time of arrival from the road of the first lay-up train, there was an interval of _____ minutes.

    A. 32   B. 35   C. 36   D. 39

11.____

12. The total number of all cars taken out of service during the period covered by the portion of the train register sheet shown was

    A. 18   B. 22   C. 30   D. 52

12.____

13. The MINIMUM layover time scheduled for any of the trains shown as arriving from Town Circle and remaining in passenger service was _____ minutes.

    A. 2   B. 6   C. 7   D. 8

13.____

14. A good average schedule speed for the type of local service indicated on the train register sheet is 15 miles per hour. If this value of schedule speed applies to the Topside locals, the distance from Upper Road to Town Circle MUST be approximately _____ miles.

    A. 10   B. 13   C. 16   D. 18

14.____

15. A passenger who wished to transfer to a northbound Bee Line train with a minimum amount of waiting time at Exchange Place boarded a northbound Topside local at Broad Boulevard. If the said Bee Line train was scheduled to leave Exchange Place at 8:31, the passenger should have boarded the train which left Broad Boulevard at

    A. 7:57   B. 7:59   C. 8:01   D. 8:03

15.____

16. With respect to yard motorman Blanc, the time interval between his arrival at Upper Road with a put-in from the yard and his departure with a lay-up for the yard was _____ minutes.

    A. 16   B. 25   C. 26   D. 29

16.____

17. The one of the following trains which MOST probably arrived at Upper Road carrying no passengers was the one scheduled to leave at

    A. 8:00   B. 8:04   C. 8:09   D. 8:20

17.____

18. When the train leaving Upper Road at 8:00 arrived at Town Circle, the LONGEST stop it could have been allowed to make without interfering with the normal movement and sequence of trains was _____ minutes.

    A. 4   B. 5   C. 8   D. 10

18.____

19. On the return trip to Upper Road, the head car of the train in Question 18 above was

    A. 79   B. 80   C. 42   D. 28

19.____

20. The train in Question 18 above could have made a reasonable stop at Town Circle and returned to Upper Road at

    A. 8:45   B. 8:53   C. 9:46   D. 9:52

20.____

21. The average scheduled time per station from Upper Road to Town Circle is 1 minute and _____ seconds.

    A. 21   B. 26   C. 39   D. 58

21.____

22. Assuming that crews have a relay of 8 to 10 minutes at Upper Road, the number of the car from which motorman Fast operated when coming into the terminal was

    A. 33   B. 130   C. 151   D. 109

22.____

23. At 8:50, the train dispatcher at Upper Road received an important message for trainman Steel. He probably could have relayed the message to Steel earliest through the train dispatcher at

    A. New Street, Steel being on a southbound trip
    B. Broad Boulevard, Steel being on a southbound trip
    C. Town Circle
    D. Broad Boulevard, Steel being on a northbound trip

23.____

24. A passenger for Town Circle arrived at Exchange Place at 8:05 and, finding the southbound trains very crowded, decided to ride to Upper Road to get a seat on a southbound train. The EARLIEST he could have arrived at Town Circle was

    A. 903   B. 907   C. 913   D. 920

24.____

25. At 8:30 the train which left Upper Road at 8:04 was between

    A. Exchange Place and Old Avenue
    B. Old Avenue and New Street
    C. New Street and Broad Blvd.
    D. Broad Blvd. and Town Circle

25.____

26. At 8:15 the train which arrived at Upper Road at 8:46 was 　　　　26._____

    A. between Broad Blvd. and New Street
    B. at New Street
    C. between New Street and Old Avenue
    D. at Old Avenue

27. The symbol 　　　　　　near New Street on the diagram represents 　　27._____

    A. a turnout
    B. a diamond crossover
    C. two turnouts and a storage track
    D. a switchback or tail track

28. The PROPER time for the conductor of a northbound Topside Local to change the rear 　　28._____
markers on his train is

    A. after coming to a stop at Upper Road
    B. any time there is an opportunity one or two stations before Upper Road
    C. while on the crossover entering Upper Road
    D. just before leaving Exchange Place

29. If the train dispatcher at Exchange Place notices a white marker light on the rear of a 　　29._____
southbound Topside Local, his proper move is to

    A. notify the trainmaster
    B. notify the train dispatcher at Upper Road and the train dispatcher at Town Circle
    C. notify the assistant train dispatcher at Old Avenue and the motorman of the follow-
ing train
    D. note the details on his gap sheet but take no other action

30. A *run number* refers to 　　　　30._____

    A. the number of trains that have left a terminal, counting from midnight
    B. a particular tour of duty for a train crew
    C. a particular train for the period it is in passenger service
    D. the leading car number of a train leaving a south terminal

31. Three yellow lanterns hung one above the other adjacent to a track mean 　　31._____

    A. stop and then proceed
    B. speed limit is 10 M.P.H.
    C. telephone for orders
    D. broken rail

32. A proceed hand signal can be given with a lantern whose color is 　　32._____

    A. red or white   B. yellow or green
    C. yellow or red   D. any of the above

33. In order to guard against improper functioning of the signal system, the rules require flags to be set out when moving a train

    A. to the express track from the local track
    B. from the express track to the local track
    C. against traffic beyond interlocking limits
    D. into the shop from a yard lay-up track

33._____

34. A train dispatcher knows the car inspector is wanted when he hears the whistle

    A. 00   B. - - 00   C. - -   D. 000

34._____

35. One function of the emergency alarm system in the subway is to

    A. start emergency exhaust fans
    B. sound an emergency alarm in the nearest fire house
    C. connect the adjacent telephone to the emergency switchboard
    D. provide emergency power for signals

35._____

36. A two-part tour of duty having a break between the two parts of less than one hour is a _____ trick.

    A. swing   B. straight   C. relay   D. split

36._____

37. A railroad clerk whose normal tour of duty is from 12:00 midnight to 8:00 A.M. and whose regular days off are Saturday and Sunday is notified to appear to take a written test for promotion to Assistant Train Dispatcher on Saturday, April 27th, at 9:30 A.M. According to the rules, this man should be

    A. required to work a P.M. trick on Saturday
    B. excused from his Friday tour but required to work on Sunday
    C. excused from his Friday tour with pay
    D. required to work all his regular tricks

37._____

38. The LEAST effective way to reduce the employee accident rate in the subways is to

    A. display new safety posters frequently
    B. offer prizes for the best safety records
    C. have employees attend regular safety instruction classes
    D. let employees learn through their own mistakes

38._____

39. Supervisors are required to make reports on each employee accident in addition to the reports of the injured employee and the witnesses. Of the following entries, the one MOST useful on the supervisor's report is the

    A. name of the injured employee
    B. names of witnesses
    C. cause of the accident
    D. location of the accident

39._____

40. If the headway on a particular track is alternately 1 1/2 minutes and 3 1/2 minutes between successive trains, the number of trains per hour will be

    A. 8   B. 12   C. 17   D. 24

40._____

41. During rush hours, a person wishing to travel from West 42nd Street, Manhattan, to South Ferry without changing trains could use the   41.____

    A.   IRT-7th Ave. Express
    B.   IND-8th Ave. Local
    C.   BMT-Broadway (Manhattan) Local
    D.   IND-6th Ave. Express

42. Tail lights carried on the rear ends of passenger trains are located at the   42.____

    A.   top, right, and left
    B.   bottom, right, and left
    C.   top and bottom, right side
    D.   top and bottom, left side

43. When single-track is operated in an under-river tunnel, it is usually in accordance with a prepared supplementary timetable. Such supplementary timetables are prepared by   43.____

    A.   trainmasters   B.   dispatchers
    C.   schedule makers   D.   station supervisors

44. After snow begins to fall, towermen in yards are expected to   44.____

    A.   operate switches and signals frequently
    B.   clamp all switches on storage tracks
    C.   report weather conditions to the trainmaster at regular intervals
    D.   make all snow removal equipment readily accessible

45. If only one crew out of your terminal was always behind schedule, this could NOT be entirely due to   45.____

    A.   slow door operation
    B.   too much coasting
    C.   braking too soon and too slowly
    D.   faulty car equipment

46. Assistant train dispatchers are NOT stationed in the   46.____

    A.   trainmasters' offices
    B.   crew dispatchers' offices
    C.   signal towers
    D.   crew rooms

47. Longer trains on a shorter headway than called for by the regular timetables have often been operated during snowfalls in the middle of the day. The PRIMARY purpose of such operation has been to   47.____

    A.   prevent jamming of doors
    B.   avoid having trains snowbound in yards
    C.   carry the increased passenger load
    D.   keep yard tracks clear of snow

48. Trains were recently rerouted in a subway section to permit repairs to the *track invert*.   48.____
    These repairs were made to the

    A. running rails
    C. subway roof
    B. subway floor
    D. bench walk

49. Of the following, the LEAST likely cause of an accident in a dispatcher's office is   49.____

    A. more than one job at a time on the desk
    B. an open file drawer
    C. discarded cigarette butts on the floor
    D. electrical extension cords strung across the floor

50. The first of three storage tracks holds as many cars as the other two together, and the   50.____
    second holds twice as many cars as the third. If the first track holds 30 cars, the first and
    third tracks together hold _____ cars.

    A. 60   B. 50   C. 45   D. 40

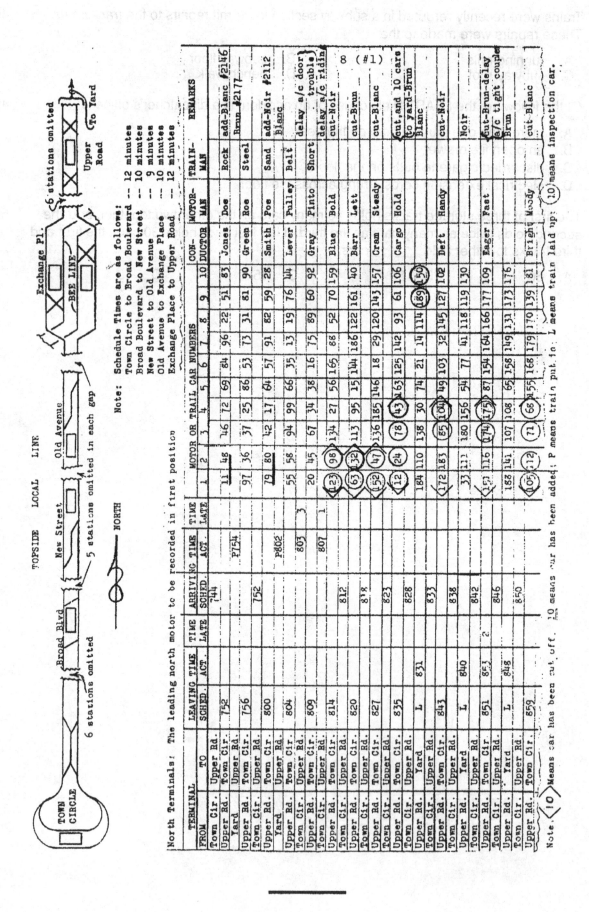

KEY (CORRECT ANSWERS)

1. A	11. A	21. C	31. B	41. C
2. D	12. D	22. C	32. B	42. B
3. B	13. D	23. C	33. C	43. C
4. B	14. B	24. C	34. D	44. A
5. A	15. C	25. B	35. A	45. D
6. A	16. D	26. B	36. B	46. D
7. B	17. B	27. C	37. D	47. B
8. D	18. C	28. A	38. D	48. C
9. A	19. D	29. C	39. C	49. A
10. C	20. D	30. B	40. D	50. D

TEST 2

DIRECTIONS: Each question or incomplete statement is followed by several suggested answers or completions. Select the one that BEST answers the question or completes the statement. *PRINT THE LETTER OF THE CORRECT ANSWER IN THE SPACE AT THE RIGHT.*

1. The last rapid transit tunnel from Manhattan to Queens has its Manhattan end at approximately _____ Street.   1.____

    A. 76th   B. 69th   C. 63rd   D. 57th

2. The Franklin Avenue-Prospect Park shuttle in Brooklyn provides free interchange of passengers between the   2.____

    A. Broadway (Brooklyn) line of the BMT Division and the Rockaway line
    B. Eastern Parkway line of the IRT Division and the West End line of the BMT Division
    C. Culver line of the IND Division and the Brighton line of the BMT Division
    D. Brighton line of the BMT Division and the Fulton St. line of the IND Division

3. Subway interconnections now in operation permit the operation of _____ , Manhattan   3.____

    A. Broadway, Brooklyn, trains on 6th Avenue
    B. Flushing, Queens, trains on Lexington Avenue
    C. Astoria, Queens, trains on 8th Avenue
    D. Woodlawn, Bronx, trains on 7th Avenue

4. The 42nd Street shuttle in Manhattan provides free interchange of passengers between the   4.____

    A. Jamaica line of the BMT Division and the Van Cortlandt Park line of the IRT Division
    B. 6th and 8th Avenue lines of the IND Division
    C. Lexington Ave. line of the IRT Division and the 8th Ave. line of the IND Division
    D. Lexington Ave. line of the IRT Division and the Broadway subway of the BMT Division

5. Train register sheets are kept MAINLY at   5.____

    A. road car inspectors' headquarters
    B. intermediate time points
    C. yardmasters' offices
    D. main line terminals

6. Car defect sheets are GENERALLY provided at   6.____

    A. home terminals
    B. junction signal towers
    C. gap station dispatchers' offices
    D. road car inspectors' headquarters

7. Gap sheets are sometimes maintained by   7.____

    A. motormen   B. road trainmasters
    C. towermen   D. platformmen

8. Trains of a certain two-track line without branch lines are scheduled to leave the home terminal at 11:03, 11:09, 11:15, 11:21, 11:27, 11:33, and 11:39. After the 11:03 has left, it is found that the train scheduled to leave at 11:09 must be taken out of service and no replacement can be obtained. The BEST times at which to dispatch the next 4 trains, in accordance with good rapid transit practice, are

    A. 11:08, 11:15, 11:21, 11:27
    B. 11:10, 11:17, 11:25, 11:32
    C. 11:11, 11:18, 11:24, 11:30
    D. 11:12, 11:21, 11:30, 11:39

8.____

9. Timetables are often made up so that at express stations certain local and express trains are scheduled to arrive at the same time. From the passenger's viewpoint, it is MOST important for timetables to schedule such arrivals when the

    A. headways are short
    B. express stations are far apart
    C. local stations are close together
    D. headways are long

9.____

10. If the running time between the two interlocking towers at the ends of a certain tunnel is three minutes, the minimum headway that can be achieved in one direction when single-tracking is operated with alternate trains going in opposite directions is NEAREST to _____ minutes.

    A. 3   B. 6   C. 9   D. 12

10.____

11. The interval between the time a train crew arrives at a terminal from the road and the time the same crew leaves the terminal for the road is CORRECTLY referred to as _____ time.

    A. clearing   B. interval   C. layover   D. relief

11.____

12. Short line operations means

    A. taking trains out of service as traffic decreases
    B. changing crews at gap stations
    C. running less than maximum-length trains
    D. turning trains back at intermediate terminals

12.____

13. Flexible intervals are operated when

    A. scheduled headway changes occur
    B. there has been a long delay
    C. extra trains are run for sporting events
    D. holidays occur on weekends

13.____

14. Providing the operating personnel for extra trains is the responsibility of the

    A. general superintendent
    B. desk trainmaster
    C. crew dispatcher
    D. yardmaster

14.____

15. On interlocking machines that have levers which are pushed-and-pulled, or swung from side-to-side, a single lever is NOT used to control

    A. a crossover
    B. a signal
    C. a signal and a switch
    D. the direction of traffic

15.____

16. Setting up a route on a *route interlocking* control board requires the operator to

    A. operate a switch control and then a signal control
    B. operate a signal control and then a switch control
    C. push an exit button and then an entrance button
    D. push an entrance button and then an exit button

16.____

17. In keeping train records at a terminal, it is NOT necessary for the train dispatcher to record the

    A. number of every car in each arriving and leaving train
    B. names of the motorman and conductor of each train
    C. track on which each train enters the terminal
    D. time of arrival and departure of each train

17.____

18. Protective flags or lanterns must be set out when a passenger train is to move over an infrequently used crossover because the

    A. towerman needs time to set up the route
    B. condition of the rails may result in improper signal operation
    C. condition of the track may result in flat wheels
    D. motorman might otherwise operate too fast

18.____

19. General orders of the transportation department, which are posted in the No. 1 position on all official bulletin boards, are printed on paper which is

    A. white   B. blue   C. green   D. pink

19.____

20. The notation P shown on a timetable next to the scheduled leaving time of a train denotes that the

    A. train is placed in passenger service at the point indicated
    B. road crew is changed at the point shown
    C. train is scheduled to pass certain specified stations without stopping
    D. passengers may transfer to another route at this point

20.____

Questions 21-30.

DIRECTIONS: Questions 21 through 30 are based on the following description of a special event. Refer to this description in answering these questions.

     A parade on a widely observed holiday is to follow a line of march crossing the Speed Ave. rapid transit line (a 4-track line) as shown in the sketch below; approximately 1 1/2 million spectators are anticipated. The parade will take 5 hours to pass any given point on its route, and it will take 2 hours and 15 minutes for any part of the parade to march from the beginning to the end of the . route, starting near Spring St. station at noon, marching north, and finishing near Space St. station. The nearest express terminal of the rapid transit line is 22 minutes' riding time from Space St. and the other terminal is 26 minutes' riding time from Spring St. The scheduled riding time between Space and Spring Sts. is 17 minutes via local and 12 minutes via express.

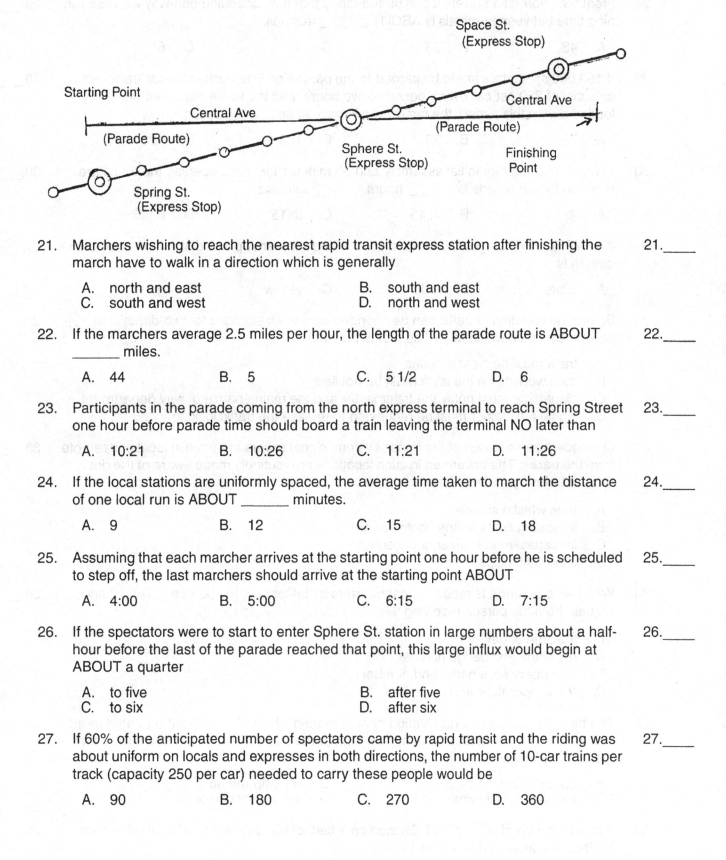

21. Marchers wishing to reach the nearest rapid transit express station after finishing the march have to walk in a direction which is generally

    A. north and east
    B. south and east
    C. south and west
    D. north and west

21.____

22. If the marchers average 2.5 miles per hour, the length of the parade route is ABOUT _____ miles.

    A. 44
    B. 5
    C. 5 1/2
    D. 6

22.____

23. Participants in the parade coming from the north express terminal to reach Spring Street one hour before parade time should board a train leaving the terminal NO later than

    A. 10:21
    B. 10:26
    C. 11:21
    D. 11:26

23.____

24. If the local stations are uniformly spaced, the average time taken to march the distance of one local run is ABOUT _____ minutes.

    A. 9
    B. 12
    C. 15
    D. 18

24.____

25. Assuming that each marcher arrives at the starting point one hour before he is scheduled to step off, the last marchers should arrive at the starting point ABOUT

    A. 4:00
    B. 5:00
    C. 6:15
    D. 7:15

25.____

26. If the spectators were to start to enter Sphere St. station in large numbers about a half-hour before the last of the parade reached that point, this large influx would begin at ABOUT a quarter

    A. to five
    B. after five
    C. to six
    D. after six

26.____

27. If 60% of the anticipated number of spectators came by rapid transit and the riding was about uniform on locals and expresses in both directions, the number of 10-car trains per track (capacity 250 per car) needed to carry these people would be

    A. 90
    B. 180
    C. 270
    D. 360

27.____

28. From the information given, it can be reasoned that the scheduled one-way express running time between terminals is ABOUT _____ minutes.

   A. 48   B. 53   C. 60   D. 65   28.____

29. If 150,000 spectators are to be carried to the parade on one track in 10-car trains with a capacity of 250 per car over a period of two hours, and the trains are about uniformly loaded during this period, the headway will have to be _____ seconds.

   A. 75   B. 90   C. 105   D. 120   29.____

30. Allowing one hour for initial assembly and 30 minutes for final dispersal, the total time required for the parade is _____ hours, _____ minutes.

   A. 7; 15   B. 7; 45   C. 8; 15   D. 8; 45   30.____

31. It is IMPROPER to signal a motorman by moving a lantern up and down if the color of the lantern is

   A. white   B. red   C. yellow   D. green   31.____

32. Before the direction of traffic can be changed on a track signaled for two-directional traffic, one condition which MUST be met is that the

   A. track must be clear of trains
   B. men working on the track must be notified
   C. dispatcher must notify the trainmaster and the maintenance of way department
   D. signal maintainer must be requested to release the traffic locking

   32.____

33. On modernized sections of the transit system, signal towers are often in locations remote from the tracks. The towermen in such locations are routinely made aware of the destinations of trains by means of the

   A. train whistle signals
   B. indicating lights on the control board
   C. loudspeaker system announcements
   D. automatic dispatcher

   33.____

34. When an oral report is made to headquarters by telephone, the person making it should request from the person receiving it

   A. the time of day
   B. his name and badge number
   C. his supervisor's name and number
   D. the temperature and humidity

   34.____

35. The train dispatcher at a gap station hears the train whistle signal 0-0-0 repeated three times as an express train is coming to a stop at the station. The dispatcher knows that this is a signal for

   A. police assistance   B. a platformman
   C. the signal maintainer   D. the car inspector

   35.____

36. Trains made up of IND or BMT Division cars cannot be operated on IRT Division lines MAINLY because of differences in

   A. height   B. length   C. width   D. weight   36.____

37. The dispatcher at a subway gap station may have to see that two flagging lanterns at his location are lighted and ready for use at all times. The colors of these lanterns are   37.____

    A. red and white   B. white and yellow
    C. yellow and green   D. green and red

38. If 40 trains per hour are operated on a certain track, the average headway is _____ seconds.   38.____

    A. 60   B. 75   C. 90   D. 105

39. Trains on a certain track operate on a 2-minute headway at a speed of 30 miles per hour. A correct expression for calculating the number of feet of distance between the front of one train and the front of the train ahead when both trains are running at the given speed is   39.____

    A. 30/60 x 2 x 5280   B. 2/30 x 60 x 5280
    C. 30/60 x 1/2 x 5280   D. 30/2 x 1/60 x 5280

40. Motormen are permitted to *economize* on time when it can be done safely after a delay. In order to save one minute on a one-mile stretch for which the timetable schedules an average speed of 15 miles per hour, the motormen would have to average _____ M.P.H.   40.____

    A. 17   B. 20   C. 22   D. 25

41. The official who, in practice, GENERALLY authorizes the operation of extra trains for special events is the   41.____

    A. central control supervisor
    B. desk trainmaster
    C. train dispatcher
    D. assistant general superintendent

42. If a motorman reports to the train dispatcher at a gap station that he has just passed a small fire between the rails on the adjacent track, the train dispatcher should FIRST   42.____

    A. operate the emergency alarm
    B. send a platformman with a portable extinguisher to the location
    C. notify the trainmaster's office
    D. contact the track department

43. Before leaving a terminal, and after receiving the indication light, a motorman is required to wait for the conductor's proceed buzzer signal. The purpose of this requirement is to be sure that the   43.____

    A. conductor is on board
    B. train dispatcher has time to make the proper entries
    C. train does not leave ahead of schedule time
    D. train line electrical circuits are complete

44. Single-track operation is GENERALLY necessary when   44.____

    A. a train with locked brakes blocks a main line in Manhattan
    B. signal cables are being replaced in an under-river tunnel
    C. running rails are being renewed in an express station
    D. lightbulbs are being replaced in an under-river tunnel

45. The train dispatcher at a gap station is told by a motorman that he passed an automatic signal with a broken lens several stations back, the motorman identifying the signal by number. The BEST immediate corrective action is to

    A. tell the motorman to call the signal office when he reaches the terminal
    B. record the information and forward it with his daily reports
    C. telephone the information to the trainmaster's office and notify the signal maintainer
    D. telephone this information to the preceding gap station and notify the section dispatcher

45.____

46. The BEST way for an assistant train dispatcher to acquaint himself with new regulations as soon as possible is to

    A. carefully read all bulletins as issued
    B. study the book of rules
    C. be alert to the needs of the service
    D. obey the orders given by the train dispatcher

46.____

47. The train breakdown which will probably cause the LONGEST delay to a 10-car train is a single

    A. grounded shoe beam
    B. blown main fuse
    C. side door that does not close
    D. burned out motorman's indication lightbulb

47.____

48. If the distance between two terminals is 8.3 miles, then a train which made 6 roundtrips traveled about _____ miles.

    A. 50   B. 65   C. 85   D. 100

48.____

49. A certain subway line has been extended to include five more local stations. Assuming that the schedule time for each local run averages 1 1/2 minutes, the number of minutes that should be added to the scheduled roundtrip time due to this extension is NEAREST to _____ minutes.

    A. 7 1/2   B. 10   C. 12 1/2   D. 15

49.____

50. After a train dispatcher pulls an emergency alarm for any reason, the NEXT move he is required by the rules to make is to notify the

    A. power dispatcher
    B. transit police
    C. track maintenance department
    D. trainmaster's office

50.____

KEY (CORRECT ANSWERS)

1.	C	11.	C	21.	C	31.	B	41.	D
2.	D	12.	D	22.	C	32.	A	42.	C
3.	A	13.	B	23.	B	33.	B	43.	A
4.	D	14.	C	24.	B	34.	B	44.	B
5.	D	15.	C	25.	A	35.	D	45.	C
6.	A	16.	D	26.	C	36.	C	46.	A
7.	C	17.	C	27.	A	37.	A	47.	A
8.	B	18.	B	28.	C	38.	C	48.	D
9.	D	19.	D	29.	D	39.	A	49.	D
10.	B	20.	A	30.	D	40.	B	50.	D

EXAMINATION SECTION
TEST 1

DIRECTIONS: Each question or incomplete statement is followed by several suggested answers or completions. Select the one that BEST answers the question or completes the statement. *PRINT THE LETTER OF THE CORRECT ANSWER IN THE SPACE AT THE RIGHT.*

1. Train register sheets are prepared at terminals on a 24-hour basis and are used for several purposes. Following are four possible uses of train register sheets which might be correct:
They are used
      I.   to maintain accurate and permanent records of train and employee movements
     II.   to determine car mileage
   III.   as official documents in possible court actions
   IV.   as statistical records for future reference Which of the following choices lists all of the above uses that are correct and lists none that is incorrect?

    A. I, II, III   B. I, II, IV
    C. I, III, IV   D. I, II, III, IV

1.____

2. The method used to take a work train from in front of an interval and place it behind that interval is called a

    A. cut   B. drop back   C. one ahead   D. relay

2.____

3. When a train is *in the hole,* it means that the

    A. train is in a station pocket
    B. train is at one of its terminal stations
    C. train has been cut out of service
    D. brakes have been applied in emergency

3.____

4. On a train register sheet, a circle drawn around a car number means that the car

    A. is a bad order car
    B. has been cut from the train
    C. is due for an inspection
    D. has been added to the train

4.____

5. The summary of Car trips form is used by the mileage department as a crosscheck of the mileage data cards, and lists all the following information EXCEPT

    A. scheduled number of car trips
    B. actual number of car trips
    C. difference between scheduled and actual number of car trips
    D. car numbers

5.____

6. When recording car numbers on train register sheets, the car number that should be recorded in the first position is the number of the leading _____ motor at _____ terminals.

    A. south; north   B. north; north
    C. south; both   D. north; south

6.____

7. Of the following categories of information, the one that is NOT normally recorded on train   7.____
interval sheets is

   A. leading car number of each train
   B. names and pass numbers of train crews
   C. adjustments to scheduled headways
   D. actual arrival times

8. The type of track that consists of two continuous ribbons of concrete on either side of a   8.____
concrete trough onto which the running rails are laid, with rubber padding between the
concrete and the rails, is type

   A. 1   B. 2   C. 3   D. 8

9. The headway on a certain line is 7 minutes.   9.____
How many additional cars are required to increase the present 6-car service on this
line to 8-car service if the running time from terminal to terminal is 1 hour and 5 minutes and the respective relay times are 6 minutes and 11 minutes?

   A. 26   B. 40   C. 42   D. 44

10. The twenty-four hour disposition sheet, which is prepared by terminal supervision, is   10.____
used PRIMARILY

   A. as a guide for day-to-day operations
   B. to indicate changes due to scheduled inspections, bad order cars, and crippled
      trains
   C. to designate replacement personnel for absent employees
   D. as a permanent record of special orders and unusual occurrences

11. Following are four statements which might be correct concerning the operation of flexible   11.____
intervals:
    I. Schedule adjustment by means of flexible intervals must in all cases be initi-
      ated and reported to tap points and the command center after no more than
      two flexed intervals have left the terminal
    II. When the adjusted interval equals the next scheduled interval, the interval
      not operated must be shown as abandoned
    III. All abandoned intervals must be clearly identified to all gap points, including
       towers, and must be carried on all train interval sheets and train register
       sheets
    IV. Any extra trains at the terminal due to earlier schedule adjustments or aban-
       donments must be removed from the station area and laid up until after the
       period of maximum headway
Which of the following choices lists all of the above statements that are correct and
none that is incorrect?

   A. I, II   B. I, III   C. II, III   D. III, IV

12. Of the following categories of information, the one that is NOT normally recorded on the yard movement sheets is   12.____

    A. scheduled arrival and departure times
    B. track numbers involved in each move
    C. disposition of cars in each move
    D. points of origin and destination of all trains entering or leaving the yard

13. A train has been involved in a collision and is now ready to be moved to a yard. However, before this train can be moved to the yard, authorization for the move must be given by which one of the following supervisors on the scene?   13.____

    A. Car maintenance supervisor
    B. Motorman instructor
    C. Zone trainmaster
    D. Superintendent, maintenance of way

14. If a train dispatcher notices that a portable fire extinguisher is missing from its location in his assigned area, he should IMMEDIATELY notify the   14.____

    A. desk trainmaster
    B. telephone subdivision of the maintenance of way department
    C. signal division of the maintenance of way department
    D. appropriate zone trainmaster

15. When a motorman operates a train from a car other than the front car, communication between the flagman at the front of the train and the motorman must be made by means of   15.____

    A. the train buzzer system
    B. sound-powered telephone
    C. hand signals
    D. the train public address system

16. Automatic signals are controlled by the movement of trains across   16.____

    A. bootlegs   B. insulated joints
    C. signal bonds   D. negative rail bonds

17. Following are four statements which might be correct concerning car trips report cards: 17.____
    I. Buff cards are used for Saturday, Sunday, and holiday schedules
    II. White cards are used when a daily schedule is in operation
    III. Each card represents one train and records the number of trips that the train makes from the home terminal on a single motorman's shift
    IV. A new card is required whenever the length of a train is changed or when a substitute car is placed into the train consist
Which of the following choices lists all of the above statements that are correct and none that is incorrect?

    A. I, II   B. I, III   C. II, IV   D. III, IV

18. The arrangement of switches which allows the MOST flexibility for train moves from one to the other of two parallel tracks is termed a   18.____

    A. turnout   B. diamond crossover
    C. crossover   D. turn in

Questions 19-22.

DIRECTIONS: Questions 19 through 20 apply to the type of signal system that is used on the BMT and IND lines and most of the IRT lines.

19. The signal aspect for a *call-on* is   19.____

    A. yellow over yellow over yellow
    B. red over red over yellow
    C. yellow over yellow over green
    D. red over red over red

20. The signal aspect which means *proceed on diverging route and be prepared to stop at the next signal* is   20.____

    A. yellow over yellow   B. green over yellow
    C. yellow over green   D. yellow over red

21. A type of signal which displays either two horizontal lunar white lights or two horizontal red lights is called a _____ signal.   21.____

    A. train order   B. train identity
    C. gap filler   D. yard indication

22. The signal aspect which permits a slow-speed train movement past the signal into a yard is yellow over   22.____

    A. yellow over lunar white   B. yellow
    C. green over yellow   D. yellow over yellow

23. Following are four statements concerning repeater signals which might be correct: 23.____
    I. A repeater signal is placed on the same side of the track as the controlling signal
    II. A repeater signal is placed on the opposite side of the track from the controlling signal
    III. Some repeater signals have automatic stop arms
    IV. A repeater signal is used to repeat the aspect of the controlling signal for greater range of vision
Which of the following choices lists all of the above statements that are correct and lists none that are incorrect?

    A. I, III   B. II, III   C. II, IV   D. II, III, IV

24. On the *A Division*, the northbound express track and the southbound express track are numbered, respectively,   24.____

    A. 4 and 3   B. 3 and 4   C. 2 and 3   D. 3 and 2

25. A road motorman, paid $20.10 an hour, reports for work on Wednesday at 7:30 A.M. and 25.____
normally clears at 3:00 P.M. What is his gross pay for the day if he is required to write an
unusual occurrence report at the end of this run?

    A. $157.80   B. $160.80   C. $170.85   D. $180.90

KEY (CORRECT ANSWERS)

1.	B	11.	C
2.	D	12.	A
3.	B	13.	A
4.	C	14.	A
5.	D	15.	B
6.	B	16.	B
7.	B	17.	C
8.	D	18.	B
9.	C	19.	B
10.	A	20.	A

21. A
22. D
23. C
24. D
25. C

TEST 2

DIRECTIONS: Each question or incomplete statement is followed by several suggested answers or completions. Select the one that BEST answers the question or completes the statement. *PRINT THE LETTER OF THE CORRECT ANSWER IN THE SPACE AT THE RIGHT.*

1. A conductor assigned to train service reports to work at 9:30 A.M. on a Friday morning wearing a uniform that is very badly soiled. The conductor's supervisor should not allow him to work, but should send him to the

   A. uniform distribution room
   B. desk trainmaster
   C. division superintendent's office
   D. chief motorman instructor

   1.____

2. A motorman of an 8-car train is told that power will be off for at least another 45 minutes while his train is stopped in the *power off* area. The motorman must apply hand brakes on _____ of his train.

   A. at least 1 car at each end
   B. at least 3 cars
   C. at least 4 cars
   D. all the cars

   2.____

3. What is the MINIMUM number of lamps required in front of a work area where normal track conditions permit train speeds in excess of 35 miles per hour?

   A. 4   B. 5   C. 6   D. 7

   3.____

4. The marking A4 564 on a signal survey plate means *A* tracks, northbound _____ feet from survey number 0 at the south end of the line.

   A. local, 56,400   B. express, 56,400
   C. local, 5,640   D. express, 5,640

   4.____

5. Following are four statements which might be correct concerning the movement of trains:
   I. A train must not go faster than 10 miles per hour coming into a terminal track ending in a bumper block
   II. A train must not go faster than 35 miles per hour in a river tunnel
   III. A train must never go faster than 10 miles per hour when moving to the left or right over a switch
   IV. A work train must not go faster than 25 miles per hour on curves

   Which of the following choices lists all of the above statements that are correct and none that is incorrect?

   A. I, II   B. I, III   C. I, IV   D. II, III

   5.____

6. The piece of equipment on a subway car which insulates the contact shoe from the track is called the

   A. emergency contactor   B. shoe beam
   C. coupler   D. contact shoe slipper

   6.____

7. A motorman who has stopped his train in a work area receives a *Proceed* signal from a   7.____
flagman using the wrong color lamp. The PROPER action for the motorman to take is to

    A. proceed with caution and be prepared to stop
    B. proceed at normal speed
    C. contact the command center
    D. question the flagman

8. On trains with *married-pair* cars, the motor-generators are located   8.____

    A. on even-numbered cars *only*
    B. on odd-numbered cars *only*
    C. at the middle of each car
    D. under each cab of each car

9. A tower horn signal consisting of one long blast means that   9.____

    A. the road car inspector should contact the tower
    B. the signal maintainer should contact the tower
    C. all trains in the interlocking limits must come to an immediate stop
    D. all trains in the interlocking limits can proceed

10. A train horn signal consisting of three short blasts   10.____

    A. is an answer to any signal
    B. is sounded when passing caution lights
    C. means that the train needs a road car inspector
    D. means that the train needs a signal maintainer

11. A *12-11* in the transportation department's radio code signal system means a situation   11.____
involving

    A. a fire   B. serious vandalism
    C. a derailment   D. a stalled train

12. A *22-6* in the transportation department's radio code signal system means a situation   12.____
involving a(n)

    A. flood   B. armed passenger
    C. passenger under a train   D. derailment

13. A supervisor makes it a practice to apply fair and firm discipline in all cases of rule infrac-   13.____
tions, including those of a minor nature.
This practice should PRIMARILY be considered

    A. *bad,* since applying discipline for minor violations is a waste of time
    B. *good,* because not applying discipline for minor infractions can lead to a more seri-
ous erosion of discipline
    C. *bad,* because employees do not like to be disciplined for minor violations of the
rules
    D. *good,* because violating any rule can cause a dangerous situation to occur

14. When a motorman stops his train so that the front car is outside the station platform, he may

    A. back up the train, provided the conductor is at the rear of the last car and has positive communication with the motorman
    B. back up the train after notifying the command center
    C. back up the train during non-rush hours if the normal headway is more than 15 minutes and if he has a flagman at the rear of the train
    D. not back up the train

14._____

15. A drum switch on a subway car affects the operation of the

    A. side doors   B. air brakes
    C. master controller   D. main car body lights

15._____

16. The schedule for a particular route indicates 20 trains per hour between 7 A.M. and 8 M. and it indicates 12 trains per hour between 9 A.M. and 10 A.M.
The average change in headway between these two time periods is _____ minutes.

    A. 2   B. 3   C. 4   D. 5

16._____

17. When a 10-car train is being prepared for service, the time allotted to the motorman to *OK* the train is generally _____ minutes.

    A. 15   B. 30   C. 45   D. 60

17._____

18. During rush hours, when scheduled headways are less than 6 minutes, holding lights may NOT be used for which of the following situations?

    A. When trains are running ahead of schedule
    B. To cover gaps or holes in service
    C. To obtain car numbers
    D. To hold trains when conditions ahead are known to prohibit movement

18._____

Questions 19-20.

DIRECTIONS: Questions 19 and 20 apply to the pushbutton type of control panel.

19. When a call-on aspect is displayed on a home signal, the associated signal indication light should be

    A. flashing yellow   B. flashing red
    C. continuous yellow   D. continuous red

19._____

20. When a signal indication light is dark, it means that there is _____ route set up and the home signal is _____.

    A. a; at *danger*   B. no; at *danger*
    C. a; *clear*   D. no; *clear*

20._____

21. When a switch is in transit, the area of the control panel showing the switch should flash

    A. green   B. white   C. C, yellow   D. red

21._____

22. Which of the following statements is TRUE about an 8-car train carrying passengers at a terminal?
    The train

    A. may leave the terminal if the air brakes are cut out on one of its cars, provided it is not the first car or the last car
    B. must not leave the terminal with the air brakes cut out on any one of its cars
    C. must not leave the terminal with the air brakes cut out on a-y one of its cars unless a motorman instructor is also on the train
    D. may leave the terminal provided the brakes are cut out on no more than two of its cars

22.____

23. If you as a supervisor find it necessary to criticize a subordinate for poor work performance, it is MOST important for you to

    A. be specific about your criticism and not to use generalities
    B. first inform the employee about the mistakes he has made in the past
    C. have witnesses present
    D. keep a record of what you are going to say to the man

23.____

24. According to Step 1 of the grievance procedure, when an aggrieved employee makes a complaint to his superior, the latter must communicate his decision to the employee within _____ after receiving the complaint.

    A. 24 hours   B. 48 hours   C. 3 days   D. 5 days

24.____

25. According to the grievance procedure, a Step 4 hearing of an aggrieved employee is conducted by the

    A. chief trainmaster
    B. superintendent of the division
    C. assistant general superintendent
    D. general superintendent

25.____

KEY (CORRECT ANSWERS)

1.	C	11.	B	21.	D
2.	C	12.	D	22.	B
3.	C	13.	B	23.	A
4.	B	14.	D	24.	B
5.	A	15.	A	25.	D
6.	B	16.	A		
7.	D	17.	C		
8.	A	18.	C		
9.	C	19.	A		
10.	C	20.	B		

TEST 3

DIRECTIONS: Each question or incomplete statement is followed by several suggested answers or completions. Select the one that BEST answers the question or completes the statement. *PRINT THE LETTER OF THE CORRECT ANSWER IN THE SPACE AT THE RIGHT.*

1. Following are four statements which might be correct concerning late departures and abandonments due to a flexible interval at terminals:
    I. Gap stations must be notified no later than two minutes after a train leaves
    II. If the lateness is due to a specific problem at the terminal, the command center must be notified
    III. No train may be abandoned to *balance service* when a crew and train are available to make the interval
    IV. When an extra train is run, it does not have to be shown as an extra train when it offsets a previously abandoned interval

   Which of the following choices lists all of the above statements that are correct and none that is incorrect?

   A. I, II   B. I, III   C. II, III   D. III, IV   1._____

2. During the rush hours at terminals, trains that are being laid up should be discharged and moved out in a period that should normally not take more than _____ minutes.   2._____

   A. 2   B. 4   C. 6   D. 8

3. When a motorman is unable to reach the command center by radio to report a temporary delay in service to his train, he SHOULD   3._____

   A. report the details of the delay to a train dispatcher or assistant train dispatcher at the next gap station he reaches and he should also request either of them to telephone the details to the command center for him
   B. contact the command center by telephone at the next gap station that he reaches to report the details of the delay
   C. contact the command center by telephone when he arrives at the terminal to report the details of the delay and he should also report the details to the train dispatcher at the terminal
   D. report the details of the delay to the train dispatcher when he arrives at the terminal and he should also request the dispatcher to telephone the details to the command center for him

4. Following are four statements which might be correct concerning the actions that a towerman must take whenever there is a switch failure and a signal maintainer is summoned: 4._____

   The towerman must
    I. establish and maintain contact with the signal maintainer so that all actions are coordinated
    II. be fully aware of the actions taken by the signal maintainer
    III. have a clear understanding with the signal maintainer regarding the position of switches in relation to the interlocking machine
    IV. observe all repairs made by the signal maintainer in the tower

Which of the following choices lists all of the above statements that are correct and none that is incorrect?

A. I, II, III
C. I, III, IV

B. I, II, III, IV
D. II, III, IV

Questions 5-7.

DIRECTIONS: Questions 5 through 7 refer to conventional (lever type) interlocking machines.

5. Traffic levers should be painted   5.____

A. blue   B. green   C. white   D. red

6. When the switch detector light is illuminated, it means that the switch   6.____

A. point is stuck
B. lever is stuck
C. is in transit
D. lever is electrically unlocked for movement

7. The switch in the sketch at the right is set for a
northbound move to Track F and
Signal 4 has been cleared for this move.
To set up a southbound move on Track E, the
PROPER sequence of interlocking machine
lever movements is   7.____

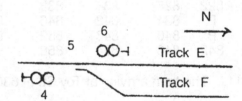

A. 4, 6, 5
B. 6, 5, 4
C. 4, 5, 6
D. 5, 4, 6

8. Employee assignment sheets are used to designate replacement personnel for absent   8.____
employees. They are prepared and issued by the

A. terminal dispatcher
C. crew dispatcher's office

B. assistant train dispatcher
D. command center

9. A light train is a train of revenue cars that   9.____

A. is being moved through a yard
B. is defective and must be taken out of service
C. has less than 8 cars
D. is being operated over main line track without passengers

10. When an emergency alarm box in a subway is operated, an '. emergency alarm recorder   10.____
will punch out on paper tape the

A. emergency alarm box number only
B. location of the emergency alarm box only
C. location of the emergency alarm box and those fans and blowers which are acti-
vated
D. emergency alarm box number and those fans and blowers which are activated

Questions 11-15.

DIRECTIONS: Questions 11 through 15 are based on the DAILY TRAIN SCHEDULE shown below. Refer to this schedule when answering these questions. Assume that all operations proceed without delay unless otherwise stated in a question.

DAILY TRAIN SCHEDULE
XX LOCAL

SOUTHBOUND							NORTHBOUND			
Elf St.		Sam St.	John St.	Boy St.	Toy St.		Boy St.	John St.	Sam St.	Elf St.
ARR	LV	LV	LV	LV	ARR	LV	LV	LV	LV	LV
700	712	720	724	730	732	742	744	750	754	802L
710	722	730	734	740	742	752	754	800	804	812
720	732	740	744	750	752	802	804	810	814	822
730	742	750	754	800	802	812	814	820	824	832L
740	752	800	804	810	812	822	824	830	834	842
P	802	810	814	820	822	832	834	840	844	852
P	810	818	822	828	830	840	842	848	852	900
812	818	826	830	836	838	848	850	856	900	908
822	826	834	838	844	846	856	858	904	908	916
P	834	842	846	852	854	904	906	912	916	924
P	840	848	852	858	900	910	912	918	922	930
842	846	854	858	904	906L					

11.   The train arriving at Toy St. at 830 is followed by the train which leaves Elf St. at   11.____

   A.   812   B.   818   C.   836   D.   840

12.   The TOTAL number of trains stopping at John St. between 752 and 848 is   12.____

   A.   6   B.   7   C.   12   D.   13

13.   Between 800 and 838, the TOTAL number of trains placed in service at Elf St. is   13.____

   A.   1   B.   2   C.   3   D.   4

14.   The TOTAL number of round trips between Elf St. and Toy St. during the period shown on the schedule is   14.____

   A.   10   B.   11   C.   12   D.   13

15.   The MINIMUM headway for trains leaving John St. in the northbound direction for the time period between 754 and 852 is _____ minutes.   15.____

   A.   4   B.   6   C.   8   D.   10

16.   An employee loading platform sign is used to designate where a train must stop so that the first door of the first car is abreast of the platform. This sign SHOULD have on it the letter(s)   16.____

   A.   E   B.   EL   C.   ELP   D.   P

17. Train dispatchers assigned to locations where emergency equipment is stored are required to check the emergency equipment   17.____

    A. twice a day   B. daily
    C. weekly   D. monthly

18. Train dispatchers should submit their bi-weekly time cards to the timekeeping office not later than _____ day(s) after the close of the payroll period.   18.____

    A. 1   B. 2   C. 3   D. 4

19. When a motorman requests a *No Lunch* allowance which cannot be verified by his field supervisor, the matter should be referred for final disposition to the   19.____

    A. chief motorman instructor
    B. desk trainmaster
    C. zone trainmaster
    D. division superintendent's office

20. The emergency team covering under-river tubes during rush hours should consist of a road car inspector   20.____

    A. and a zone trainmaster
    B. signal maintainer, and a motorman instructor
    C. and a signal maintainer
    D. and a motorman instructor

21. When single tracking is operating between two interlock-ings that have traffic control, there is need for   21.____

    A. flagging protection only
    B. a pilot only
    C. flagging protection and a pilot
    D. an absolute block

Questions 22-25.

DIRECTIONS: Questions 22 through 25 are based on the portion of a MOTORMAN'S DAILY WORK PROGRAM shown below. The right-hand portion of the work program showing TIME entries has been omitted, and you will be required to compute certain of these entries in answering the questions.

MOTORMAN'S DAILY WORK PROGRAM
POST ROAD KO LINE

NAME	PASS NO.	RUN NO.	REPORT		PUT ST.	SET ST.		PUT ST.		SET ST.		PUT ST.		RELIEVED	
			TIME	PLACE	LV	ARR	LV	ARR	LV	ARR	LV	ARR	LV	TIME	PLACE
TAB	123	104	1259 A.M.	PUT ST.	144 / 721	222 / 721	258 / 750	(404)	440) / 858	T/C			612	858	PUT ST.
LOD	678	105	129 A.M.	PUT ST.	144	252 / 736	318 / 805	(425)	500) / 912	T/C			627	912	PUT ST.
CAP	841	106	146 A.M.	PUT ST.	201	309 / 748	338 / 816	(445)	520) / 924	T/C			639	924	PUT ST.

22. The scheduled ACTUAL work time for Run No. 104 is   22._____

    A. 7 hours, 24 minutes   B. 7 hours, 44 minutes
    C. 7 hours, 59 minutes   D. 8 hours

23. The *night differential* for Run No. 104 is   23._____

    A. 0   B. 4 hours, 25 minutes
    C. 5 hours   D. 5 hours, 1 minute

24. The *boost time* for Run No. 105 is _____ minutes.   24._____

    A. 0   B. 13   C. 22   D. 33

25. If CAP, who is assigned Run No. 106, is delayed by traffic conditions so that he clears 22   25.____
    minutes late on a particular day, the number of minutes for which he will get paid at the
    rate of time and one-half on this day is _____ minutes.

    A. 0   B. 13   C. 22   D. 33

KEY (CORRECT ANSWERS)

1.	C		11.	B
2.	A		12.	D
3.	C		13.	C
4.	A		14.	B
5.	A		15.	C
6.	D		16.	D
7.	C		17.	B
8.	C		18.	C
9.	D		19.	C
10.	A		20.	D

21.	D
22.	C
23.	C
24.	B
25.	A

EXAMINATION SECTION
TEST 1

DIRECTIONS: Each question or incomplete statement is followed by several suggested answers or completions. Select the one that BEST answers the question or completes the statement. *PRINT THE LETTER OF THE CORRECT ANSWER IN THE SPACE AT THE RIGHT.*

1. A towerman, on duty, observing a person who is apparently a passenger walk off the platform onto the catwalk, should FIRST

   A. call the track department
   B. remain at his post and ignore the occurrence
   C. write down the time of the occurrence
   D. call to the person and demand identification

1.____

2. The scheduled time interval between trains is known as

   A. relay time   B. gap
   C. running time   D. headway

2.____

3. The employee in DIRECT charge of train operations in a yard is USUALLY a

   A. yardmaster   B. motorman instructor
   C. train dispatcher   D. towerman

3.____

4. One purpose of the book of *Rules and Regulations*, also referred to as the *Book of Rules*, is to

   A. show how to operate an interlocking machine
   B. give guidelines for the salaries of the operating department's employees
   C. specify the general duties of the various operating departments' employees
   D. make most of the non-supervisory jobs easily interchangeable

4.____

5. A towerman is required to submit written reports of all unusual occurrences promptly. The BEST reason for such promptness is that the

   A. report may be too long if made at his convenience
   B. towerman will not be as likely to forget to make the report
   C. report will tend to be more accurate as to facts
   D. towerman is likely to make a better report under pressure

5.____

6. The operating (desk) trainmaster's office is located at

   A. East New York   B. 370 Jay Street
   C. Times Square   D. Coney Island

6.____

7. The average speed of a train between two terminals 6 miles apart is 12 M.P.H. The time required to make one roundtrip allowing 15 minutes for relay time at the far terminal is _____ minutes.

   A. 60   B. 65   C. 70   D. 75

7.____

8. According to the rules, the making of personal telephone calls using company phones is not permitted.
   The MAIN reason for this rule is to

   A. keep the lines open in case of an emergency
   B. reduce operating expenses
   C. reduce the number of telephone operators required
   D. prevent wasted time by employees

8.____

9. On level tangent track, two yellow lanterns are placed 600 feet from a flagman guarding a work gang. According to standard flagging instructions,

   A. the lanterns are too close to the flagman
   B. the lanterns are too far away from the flagman
   C. only flags are allowed
   D. the lanterns are properly placed

9.____

10. The MAIN reason for keeping interlocking machines locked is to

    A. prevent theft
    B. keep the equipment clean
    C. prevent tampering with the equipment
    D. prevent accidental electrical shock

10.____

11. If a towerman wishes to cause all trains in the interlocking limits to come to an immediate stop, he should sound, on the tower whistle or horn, _____ blast(s).

    A. one short   B. two long   C. one long   D. two short

11.____

12. A signal that gives both route and block indication is a _____ signal.

    A. home
    C. train order
    B. dwarf
    D. marker

12.____

13. Transit employees are cautioned, as a safety measure, not to use water on electrical equipment fires, MAINLY because the water may

    A. transmit shock to the user
    B. damage the equipment
    C. cause harmful vapors
    D. spread the fire

13.____

14. When a towerman is reporting a fire by phone, it would be MOST important for him to report

    A. the time when he noticed the fire
    B. the exact location of the fire
    C. his name and pass number
    D. the cause of the fire

14.____

15. The blue lights stationed at frequent intervals in the subway ALWAYS indicate the presence of a(n)

    A. interlocking tower
    C. emergency exit
    B. home signal
    D. emergency alarm box

15.____

16. Each track of a four track lay-up yard can hold 10 cars. There are a total of 10 cars already in this yard.
The number of ADDITIONAL cars that can be stored in this yard is

    A. 35   B. 30   C. 25   D. 20

16.____

17. The color of the hand lantern NOT used to give a proceed signal is

    A. white   B. green   C. yellow   D. red

17.____

18. The towerman can use the manipulation chart to determine the

    A. correct combination of levers for a route
    B. cars to be sent to the inspection shed
    C. number of put-ins and lay-ups during his tour
    D. schedule of arriving and leaving trains

18.____

19. According to the *Book of Rules,* a towerman MUST, when required,

    A. make repairs to the interlocking machine
    B. crank switches and flag trains
    C. operate a train in non-passenger service
    D. assist a railroad clerk in selling tokens

19.____

20. A towerman assigned to an interlocking at a terminal would GENERALLY receive his orders from the

    A. signal maintainer
    B. train dispatcher
    C. assistant station supervisor
    D. motorman instructor

20.____

21. Train starting lights or holding lights are GENERALLY controlled from the

    A. station platform   B. train
    C. dispatcher's desk   D. relay room

21.____

22. When a motorman blows three short blasts of the whistle, the towerman knows the motorman is signaling for a

    A. car inspector   B. police officer
    C. signal maintainer   D. station employee

22.____

23. When in doubt as to the proper procedure to follow in an unusual situation, the towerman should FIRST consult the

    A. local train dispatcher
    B. assistant superintendent
    C. nearest station supervisor
    D. local signal maintainer

23.____

24. A towerman should check to see whether he has set up a wrong route when he hears a motorman blow _____ short whistle blast(s).

    A. 4   B. 3   C. 2   D. 1

24.____

25. A signal maintainer wants to make sure that a certain switch lever is not moved because he is working on the switch.
    In this case, the NORMAL procedure would be to have the towerman

    A. remove the lever
    B. pull the switch fuses
    C. place a lever block on the lever
    D. stand at the lever

25._____

_____

KEY (CORRECT ANSWERS)

1.	D	11.	C
2.	D	12.	A
3.	A	13.	A
4.	C	14.	B
5.	C	15.	D
6.	B	16.	B
7.	D	17.	D
8.	A	18.	A
9.	D	19.	B
10.	C	20.	B

21.	C
22.	A
23.	A
24.	A
25.	C

_____

TEST 2

DIRECTIONS: Each question or incomplete statement is followed by several suggested answers or completions. Select the one that BEST answers the question or completes the statement. *PRINT THE LETTER OF THE CORRECT ANSWER IN THE SPACE AT THE RIGHT.*

Questions 1-7.

DIRECTIONS: Questions 1 through 7 are based on the *Rose Line* timetable given below. Refer to this table when answering these questions. Assume that all operations proceed without delay unless otherwise stated in any question.

TIMETABLE - ROSE LINE
DAILY TRAIN SCHEDULE

NORTHBOUND						SOUTHBOUND				
David Pl. Lv.	Alice St. Lv.	15 Av. Lv.	St. Helena Av Lv.	Howard Terminal Arr.	St. Helena Av. Lv.	St. Helena Av. Lv.	15 Av. Lv.	Alice St. Lv.	David Arr.	Pl. Lv.
715	730	744	758	813	817	832	846	900	915	925
723	738	752	806	821	825	840	854	908	923	935
P731	746	800	814	829	833	848	902	916	931	L
739	754	808	822	837	841	856	910	924	939	945
P745	800	814	828	843	847	902	916	930	945	955
751	806	820	834	849	853	908	922	936	951	L
		P823	837	852	856	911	L925			
757	812	826	840	855	859	914	928	942	957	1005
P803	818	832	846	901	905	920	934	948	1003	L
809	824	838	852	907	911	926	940	954	1009	1020
817	832	846	900	915	919	934	L948			
P825	840	854	908	923	927	942	956	1010	1025	1035
833	848	902	916	931	935	950	1004	1018	1033	L
P841	856	910	924	939	943	958	1012	1026	1041	1050
849	904	918	932	947	951	1006	1020	1034	1049	L
857	912	926	940	955	959	1014	1028	1042	1057	1105
P905	920	934	948	1003	1007	1022	1036	1050	1105	L
915	930	944	958	1013	1017	1032	1046	1100	1115	1120

NOTES:

1. P indicates that a train is placed in service at the station where the letter P appears.

2. L indicates that a train is taken out of service at the station where the letter L appears.

1. The running time between St. Helena Ave. and Howard Terminal is _____ minutes.   1._____

    A. 15   B. 29   C. 33   D. 45

2. A passenger arrives at Howard Terminal at 852.   2._____
The EARLIEST time that he could arrive at David Pl. is

    A. 925   B. 942   C. 957   D. 1005

3. The length of time spent by each train at Howard Terminal is _____ minutes.   3.____

    A. 6   B. 4   C. 10   D. 8

4. The total roundtrip time including relay time at Howard Terminal for the train leaving   4.____
David Pl. at 849 is _____ minutes.

    A. 60   B. 200   C. 120   D. 100

5. The number of trains placed in service at David Pl. between 739 and 833 is   5.____

    A. 1   B. 2   C. 3   D. 4

6. The TOTAL number of trains taken out of service at David Pl. between 945 and 1025 is   6.____

    A. 1   B. 2   C. 3   D. 4

7. The MINIMUM headway leaving David Pl. is _____ minutes.   7.____

    A. 8   B. 3   C. 10   D. 6

Questions 8-12.

DIRECTIONS: Questions 8 through 12 are based on the system of signal indications that is used on Division B (previously BMT and IND) and most of Division A (previously IRT).

8. The signal aspect which means *proceed on main route* is   8.____

    A. yellow over yellow   B. green over yellow
    C. green over green   D. yellow over green

9. The signal aspect which means *proceed* is   9.____

    A. yellow   B. green   C. red   D. blue

10. The signal aspect which means *proceed with caution on diverging route, prepare to stop*   10.____
at next signal is

    A. yellow over green   B. green over green
    C. yellow   D. yellow over yellow

11. The signal aspect which means *proceed on diverging route* is   11.____

    A. green   B. green over green
    C. yellow over yellow   D. green over yellow

12. The signal aspect which means *stop* is   12.____

    A. green   B. blue   C. red   D. yellow

Questions 13-20.

DIRECTIONS: Questions 13 through 20 refer to the pushbutton type control panel interlocking machine.

13. The color of the line of lights which indicates that a route has been set up for an approaching train is   13.____

    A. white   B. blue   C. red   D. brown

14. The color of the line of lights which indicates that a train is occupying a route is   14.____

    A. white   B. green   C. red   D. yellow

15. A towerman knows that a call-on is being displayed if, on the control panel, the associated   15.____

    A. exit light flashes red
    B. signal indication light flashes yellow
    C. switch indicator light flashes yellow
    D. signal indication light flashes white

16. A switch in transit is indicated by a   16.____

    A. flashing yellow light
    B. flashing red light in the associated track section
    C. line of white lights
    D. line of red lights

17. To set up a route,   17.____

    A. only push the proper entrance button
    B. only push the proper exit button
    C. push the proper entrance and exit button
    D. pull the proper entrance and exit button

18. With the route set up and the train on the approach to the home signal, the call-on aspect is displayed by   18.____

    A. pushing call-on button   B. pushing entrance button
    C. pushing exit button   D. operating proper lever

19. Signal indication lights are NORMALLY   19.____

    A. blue   B. white   C. green   D. dark

20. A symbol that USUALLY appears on a control panel is a _____ symbol.   20.____

    A. blue light   B. home signal
    C. lever   D. contact rail

Questions 21-35.

DIRECTIONS: Questions 21 through 25 refer to conventional (lever type) interlocking machines.

21. In accordance with standard practice, signal levers should be painted   21.____

    A. red   B. white   C. yellow   D. black

22. In accordance with standard practice, switch levers should be painted   22.____

    A. red   B. white   C. yellow   D. black

23. In accordance with standard practice, spare levers should be painted   23.____

    A. red   B. white   C. yellow   D. black

24. In accordance with standard practice, traffic levers should be painted   24.____

    A. red   B. white   C. yellow   D. black

25. One type of track special work, which appears on some interlocking machine model boards, is called a   25.____

    A. contact rail   B. automatic signal block
    C. viaduct   D. diamond crossover

26. The FULL NORMAL position of the signal lever for a GRS, all electric, interlocking machine is   26.____

    A. pulled out   B. pushed in
    C. to the right   D. to the left

27. The FULL REVERSE position of the signal lever for a GRS, all electric, interlocking machine is   27.____

    A. pulled out   B. pushed in
    C. to the right   D. to the left

28. The FULL NORMAL position of the switch lever for a US&S, electro-pneumatic, interlocking machine is   28.____

    A. pulled out   B. pushed in
    C. to the right   D. to the left

29. The FULL REVERSE position of the switch lever for a US&S, electro-pneumatic, interlocking machine is   29.____

    A. pulled out   B. pushed in
    C. to the right   D. to the left

30. A switch lever light (also known as switch detector light) MUST be illuminated in order   30.____

    A. to operate the switch lever
    B. for alarm to sound
    C. to lock switch
    D. to operate emergency screw release

31. A *can clear light* MUST be illuminated in order to   31.____

    A. turn on the station starting lights
    B. operate the associated switch lever
    C. operate the emergency screw release
    D. clear the associated signal

32. Some tracks are signalled to allow trains to move in either direction. The direction of train movement, in these cases, is controlled by a _____ lever.   32.____

    A. switch   B. traffic   C. signal   D. stub

33. If a lever in a unit-lever interlocking machine cannot be moved to clear a signal, the towerman should FIRST   33.____

    A. call the signal maintainer for help
    B. use a little more effort to move the lever
    C. see if any model board lights are illuminated
    D. check that the proper combination of levers is set up

34. Before operating a switch by means of the emergency release, a towerman MUST   34.____

    A. crank the switch
    B. have third rail power turned off
    C. check on the location of trains
    D. operate the call-on button

35. One color NOT used to identify the levers on an interlocking machine is   35.____

    A. green   B. blue   C. black   D. yellow

KEY (CORRECT ANSWERS)

1.	A		16.	B
2.	C		17.	C
3.	B		18.	A
4.	C		19.	D
5.	C		20.	B
6.	B		21.	A
7.	D		22.	D
8.	C		23.	C
9.	B		24.	B
10.	D		25.	D
11.	D		26.	B
12.	C		27.	A
13.	A		28.	D
14.	C		29.	C
15.	B		30.	A

31.	D
32.	B
33.	D
34.	C
35.	A

---

READING COMPREHENSION
UNDERSTANDING AND INTERPRETING WRITTEN MATERIAL
EXAMINATION SECTION
TEST 1

DIRECTIONS   Each question or incomplete statement is followed by several suggested answers or completions. Select the one that BEST answers the question or completes the statement. *PRINT THE LETTER OF THE CORRECT ANSWER IN THE SPACE AT THE RIGHT.*

Questions 1-8.

DIRECTIONS: Questions 1 through 8 are to be answered on the basis of the following regulations governing Newspaper Carriers when on subway trains or station platforms. These Newspaper Carriers are issued badges which entitle them to enter subway stations, when carrying papers in accordance with these regulations, without paying a fare.

REGULATIONS GOVERNING NEWSPAPER CARRIERS WHEN ON SUBWAY TRAINS OR STATION PLATFORMS

1.   Carriers must wear badges at all times when on trains.
2.   Carriers must not sort, separate, or wrap bundles on trains or insert sections.
3.   Carriers must not obstruct platform of cars or stations.
4.   Carriers may make delivery to stands inside the stations by depositing their badge with the station agent.
5.   Throwing of bundles is strictly prohibited and will be cause for arrest.
6.   Each bundle must not be over 18" x 12" x 15".
7.   Not more than two bundles shall be carried by each carrier. (An extra fare to be charged for a second bundle.)
8.   No wire to be used on bundles carried into stations.

1.   These regulations do NOT prohibit carriers on trains from _____ newspapers.   1.____

    A. sorting bundles of   B. carrying bundles of
    C. wrapping bundles of   D. inserting sections into

2.   A carrier delivering newspapers to a stand inside of the station MUST   2.____

    A. wear his badge at all times
    B. leave his badge with the railroad clerk
    C. show his badge to the railroad clerk
    D. show his badge at the newsstand

3.   Carriers are warned against throwing bundles of newspapers from trains MAINLY because these acts may   3.____

    A. wreck the stand   B. cause injury to passengers
    C. hurt the carrier   D. damage the newspaper

4. It is permissible for a carrier to temporarily leave his bundles of newspapers   4._____

    A. near the subway car's door
    B. at the foot of the station stairs
    C. in front of the exit gate
    D. on a station bench

5. Of the following, the carrier who should NOT be restricted from entering the subway is the one carrying a bundle which is _____long, _____ wide, and _____ high.   5._____

    A. 15"; 18"; 18"   B. 18"; 12"; 18"
    C. 18"; 12"; 15"   D. 18"; 15"; 15"

6. A carrier who will have to pay one fare is carrying _____ bundle(s).   6._____

    A. one   B. two   C. three   D. four

7. Wire may NOT be used for tying bundles because it may be   7._____

    A. rusty
    B. expensive
    C. needed for other purposes
    D. dangerous to other passengers

8. If a carrier is arrested in violation of these regulations, the PROBABLE reason is that he   8._____

    A. carried too many papers
    B. was not wearing his badge
    C. separated bundles of newspapers on the train
    D. tossed a bundle of newspapers to a carrier on a train

Questions 9-12.

DIRECTIONS: Questions 9 through 12 are to be answered on the basis of the Bulletin printed below. Read this Bulletin carefully before answering these questions. Select your answers ONLY on the basis of this Bulletin.

BULLETIN

Rule 107(m) states, in part, that *Before closing doors they (Conductors) must afford passengers an opportunity to detrain and entrain...*

Doors must be left open long enough to allow passengers to enter and exit from the train. Closing doors on passengers too quickly does not help to shorten the station stop and is a violation of the safety and courtesy which must be accorded to all our passengers.

The proper and effective way to keep passengers moving in and out of the train is to use the public address system. When the train is excessively crowded and passengers on the platform are pushing those in the cars, it may be necessary to close the doors after a reasonable period of time has been allowed.

Closing doors on passengers too quickly is a violation of rules and will be cause for disciplinary actions.

9. Which of the following statements is CORRECT about closing doors on passengers too quickly? It   9.____

    A. will shorten the running time from terminal to terminal
    B. shortens the station stop but is a violation of safety and courtesy
    C. does not help shorten the station stop time
    D. makes the passengers detrain and entrain quicker

10. The BEST way to get passengers to move in and out of cars quickly is to   10.____

    A. have the platform conductors urge passengers to move into doorways
    B. make announcements over the public address system
    C. start closing doors while passengers are getting on
    D. set a fixed time for stopping at each station

11. The conductor should leave doors open at each station stop long enough for passengers to   11.____

    A. squeeze into an excessively crowded train
    B. get from the local to the express train
    C. get off and get on the train
    D. hear the announcements over the public address system

12. Closing doors on passengers too quickly is a violation of rules and is cause for   12.____

    A. the conductor's immediate suspension
    B. the conductor to be sent back to the terminal for another assignment
    C. removal of the conductor at the next station
    D. disciplinary action to be taken against the conductor

Questions 13-15.

DIRECTIONS: Questions 13 through 15 are to be answered on the basis of the Bulletin printed below. Read this Bulletin carefully before answering these questions. Select your answers ONLY on the basis of this Bulletin.

BULLETIN

Conductors assigned to train service are not required to wear uniform caps from June 1 to September 30, inclusive.

Conductors assigned to platform duty are required to wear the uniform cap at all times. Conductors are reminded that they must furnish their badge numbers to anyone who requests same.

During the above-mentioned period, conductors may remove their uniform coats. The regulation summer short-sleeved shirts must be worn with the regulation uniform trousers. Suspenders are not permitted if the uniform coat is removed. Shoes are to be black but sandals, sneakers, suede, canvas, or two-tone footwear must not be worn.

Conductors may work without uniform tie if the uniform coat is removed. However, only the top collar button may be opened. The tie may not be removed if the uniform coat is worn.

13. Conductors assigned to platform duty are required to wear uniform caps   13.____

    A. at all times except from June 1 to September 30, inclusive
    B. whenever they are on duty
    C. only from June 1 to September 30, inclusive
    D. only when they remove their uniform coats

14. Suspenders are permitted ONLY if conductors wear   14.____

    A. summer short-sleeved shirts with uniform trousers
    B. uniform trousers without belt loops
    C. the type permitted by the authority
    D. uniform coats

15. A conductor MUST furnish his badge number to   15.____

    A. authority supervisors only
    B. members of special inspection only
    C. anyone who asks him for it
    D. passengers only

Questions 16-17.

DIRECTIONS: Questions 16 and 17 are to be answered SOLELY on the basis of the following Bulletin.

BULLETIN

    Effective immediately, Conductors on trains equipped with public address systems shall make the following announcements in addition to their regular station announcement. At stations where passengers normally board trains from their homes or places of employment, the announcement shall be *Good Morning* or *Good Afternoon* or *Good Evening,* depending on the time of the day. At stations where passengers normally leave trains for their homes or places of employment, the announcement shall be *Have a Good Day* or *Good Night,* depending on the time of day or night.

16. The MAIN purpose of making the additional announcements mentioned in the Bulletin is MOST likely to   16.____

    A. keep passengers informed about the time of day
    B. determine whether the public address system works in case of an emergency
    C. make the passengers' ride more pleasant
    D. have the conductor get used to using the public address system

17. According to this Bulletin, a conductor should greet passengers boarding the *D* train at the Coney Island Station at 8 A.M. Monday by announcing   17.____

    A. Have a Good Day
    B. Good Morning
    C. Watch your step as you leave
    D. Good Evening

Questions 18-25.

DIRECTIONS: Questions 18 through 25 are to be answered on the basis of the information
                      regarding the incident given below. Read this information carefully before
                      answering these questions.

INCIDENT

As John Brown, a cleaner, was sweeping the subway station platform, in accordance with his assigned schedule, he was accused by Henry Adams of unnecessarily bumping him with the broom and scolded for doing this work when so many passengers were on the platform. Adams obtained Brown's badge number and stated that he would report the matter to the Transit Authority. Standing around and watching this were Mary Smith, a schoolteacher, Ann Jones, a student, and Joe Black, a maintainer, with Jim Roe, his helper, who had been working on one of the turnstiles. Brown thereupon proceeded to take the names and addresses of these people as required by the Transit Authority rule which directs that names and addresses of as many disinterested witnesses be taken as possible. Shortly thereafter, a train arrived at the station and Adams, as well as several other people, boarded the train and left. Brown went back to his work of sweeping the station.

18.   The cleaner was sweeping the station at this time because   18._____

      A.   the platform was unusually dirty
      B.   there were very few passengers on the platform
      C.   he had no regard for the passengers
      D.   it was set by his work schedule

19.   This incident proves that   19._____

      A.   witnesses are needed in such cases
      B.   porters are generally careless
      C.   subway employees stick together
      D.   brooms are dangerous in the subway

20.   Joe Black was a   20._____

      A.   helper   B.   maintainer
      C.   cleaner   D.   teacher

21.   The number of persons witnessing this incident was   21._____

      A. 2   B. 3   C. 4   D. 5

22.   The addresses of witnesses are required so that they may later be   22._____

      A.   depended on to testify   B.   recognized
      C.   paid   D.   located

23.   The person who said he would report this incident to the transit authority was   23._____

      A.   Black   B.   Adams   C.   Brown   D.   Roe

24. The ONLY person of the following who positively did NOT board the train was   24.____

    A. Brown   B. Smith   C. Adams   D. Jones

25. As a result of this incident,   25.____

    A. no action need be taken against the cleaner unless Adams makes a written complaint
    B. the cleaner should be given the rest of the day off
    C. the handles of the brooms used should be made shorter
    D. Brown's badge number should be changed

KEY (CORRECT ANSWERS)

1.	B		11.	C
2.	B		12.	D
3.	B		13.	B
4.	D		14.	D
5.	C		15.	C
6.	A		16.	C
7.	D		17.	B
8.	D		18.	D
9.	C		19.	A
10.	B		20.	B

21.	C
22.	D
23.	B
24.	A
25.	A

TEST 2

DIRECTIONS: Each question or incomplete statement is followed by several suggested answers or completions. Select the one that BEST answers the question or completes the statement. *PRINT THE LETTER OF THE CORRECT ANSWER IN THE SPACE AT THE RIGHT.*

Questions 1-10.

DIRECTIONS: Questions 1 through 10 are to be answered on the basis of the information contained in the following safety rules. Read the rules carefully before answering these questions.

SAFETY RULES

Employees must take every precaution to prevent accidents, or injury to persons, or damage to property. For this reason, they must observe conditions of the equipment and tools with which they work, and the structures upon which they work.

It is the duty of all employees to report to their superior all dangerous conditions which they may observe. Employees must use every precaution to prevent the origin of fire. If they discover smoke or a fire in the subway, they shall proceed to the nearest telephone and notify the trainmaster giving their name, badge number, and location of the trouble.

In case of accidents on the subway system, employees must, if possible, secure the name, address, and telephone number of any passengers who may have been injured.

Employees at or near the location of trouble on the subway system, whether it be a fire or an accident, shall render all practical assistance which they are qualified to perform.

1. The BEST way for employees to prevent an accident is to   1.____

    A. secure the names of the injured persons
    B. arrive promptly at the location of the accident
    C. give their name and badge numbers to the trainmaster
    D. take all necessary precautions

2. In case of trouble, trackmen are NOT expected to   2.____

    A. report fires
    B. give help if they don't know how
    C. secure telephone numbers of persons injured in subway accidents
    D. give their badge number to anyone

3. Trackmen MUST   3.____

    A. be present at all fires
    B. see all accidents
    C. report dangerous conditions
    D. be the first to discover smoke in the subway

4. Observing conditions means to 4.____

    A. look at things carefully
    B. report what you see
    C. ignore things that are none of your business
    D. correct dangerous conditions

5. A dangerous condition existing on the subway system which a trackman should observe and report to his superior would be 5.____

    A. passengers crowding into trains
    B. trains running behind schedule
    C. tools in defective condition
    D. some newspapers on the track

6. If a trackman discovers a badly worn rail, he should 6.____

    A. not take any action
    B. remove the worn section of rail
    C. notify his superior
    D. replace the rail

7. The MAIN reason a trackman should observe the condition of his tools is 7.____

    A. so that they won't be stolen
    B. because they don't belong to him
    C. to prevent accidents
    D. because they cannot be replaced

8. If a passenger who paid his fare is injured in a subway accident, it is MOST important that an employee obtain the passenger's 8.____

    A. name   B. age
    C. badge number   D. destination

9. An employee who happens to be at the scene of an accident on a crowded station of the system should 9.____

    A. not give assistance unless he chooses to do so
    B. leave the scene immediately
    C. question all bystanders
    D. render whatever assistance he can

10. If a trackman discovers a fire at one end of a station platform and telephones the information to the trainmaster, he need NOT give 10.____

    A. the trainmaster's name
    B. the name of the station involved
    C. his own name
    D. the number of his badge

Questions 11-15.

DIRECTIONS: Questions 11 through 15 are to be answered on the basis of the information
contained in the safety regulations given below. Refer to these rules in answering these questions.

REGULATIONS FOR SMALL GROUPS WHO
MOVE FROM POINT TO POINT ON THE TRACKS

Employees who perform duties on the tracks in small groups and who move from point to
point along the trainway must be on the alert at all times and prepared to clear the track when
a train approaches without unnecessarily slowing it down. Underground at all times, and out-
of-doors between sunset and sunrise, such employees must not enter upon the tracks unless
each of them is equipped with an approved light. Flashlights must not be used for protection
by such groups. Upon clearing the track to permit a train to pass, each member of the group
must give a proceed signal, by hand or light, to the motorman of the train. Whenever such
small groups are working in an area protected by caution lights or flags, but are not members
of the gang for whom the flagging protection was established, they must not give proceed signals to motormen. The purpose of this rule is to avoid a motorman's confusing such signal
with that of the flagman who is protecting a gang. Whenever a small group is engaged in work
of an engrossing nature or at any time when the view of approaching trains is limited by reason of curves or otherwise, one man of the group, equipped with a whistle, must be assigned
properly to warn and protect the man or men at work and must not perform any other duties
while so assigned.

11. If a small group of men are traveling along the tracks toward their work location and a   11.____
     train approaches, they should

     A.   stop the train
     B.   signal the motorman to go slowly
     C.   clear the track
     D.   stop immediately

12. Small groups may enter upon the tracks   12.____

     A.   only between sunset and sunrise
     B.   provided each has an approved light
     C.   provided their foreman has a good flashlight
     D.   provided each man has an approved flashlight

13. After a small group has cleared the tracks in an area unprotected by caution lights or   13.____
     flags,

     A.   each member must give the proceed signal to the motorman
     B.   the foreman signals the motorman to proceed
     C.   the motorman can proceed provided he goes slowly
     D.   the last member off the tracks gives the signal to the motorman

14. If a small group is working in an area protected by the signals of a track gang, the mem-   14.____
     bers of the small group

     A.   need not be concerned with train movement
     B.   must give the proceed signal together with the track gang

C. can delegate one of their members to give the proceed signal
D. must not give the proceed signal

15. If the view of approaching trains is blocked, the small group should   15.____

    A. move to where they can see the trains
    B. delegate one of the group to warn and protect them
    C. keep their ears alert for approaching trains
    D. refuse to work at such locations

Questions 16-25.

DIRECTIONS: Questions 16 through 25 are to be answered SOLELY on the basis of the article about general safety precautions given below.

GENERAL SAFETY PRECAUTIONS

When work is being done on or next to a track on which regular trains are running, special signals must be displayed as called for in the general rules for flagging. Yellow caution signals, green clear signals, and a flagman with a red danger signal are required for the protection of traffic and workmen in accordance with the standard flagging rules. The flagman shall also carry a white signal for display to the motorman when he may proceed. The foreman in charge must see that proper signals are displayed.

On elevated lines during daylight hours, the yellow signal shall be a yellow flag, the red signal shall be a red flag, the green signal shall be a green flag, and the white signal shall be a white flag. In subway sections, and on elevated lines after dark, the yellow signal shall be a yellow lantern, the red signal shall be a red lantern, the green signal shall be a green lantern, and the white signal shall be a white lantern.

Caution and clear signals are to be secured to the elevated or subway structure with non-metallic fastenings outside the clearance line of the train and on the motorman's side of the track.

16. On elevated lines during daylight hours, the caution signal is a   16.____

    A. yellow lantern   B. green lantern
    C. yellow flag   D. green flag

17. In subway sections, the clear signal is a   17.____

    A. yellow lantern   B. green lantern
    C. yellow flag   D. green flag

18. The MINIMUM number of lanterns that a subway track flagman should carry is   18.____

    A. 1   B. 2   C. 3   D. 4

19. The PRIMARY purpose of flagging is to protect the   19.____

    A. flagman   B. motorman
    C. track workers   D. railroad

20. A suitable fastening for securing caution lights to the elevated or subway structure is   20.____

    A. copper nails   B. steel wire
    C. brass rods   D. cotton twine

21. On elevated structures during daylight hours, the red flag is held by the   21.____

    A. motorman   B. foreman   C. trackman   D. flagman

22. The signal used in the subway to notify a motorman to proceed is a   22.____

    A. white lantern   B. green lantern
    C. red flag   D. yellow flag

23. The caution, clear, and danger signals are displayed for the information of   23.____

    A. trackmen   B. workmen   C. flagmen   D. motormen

24. Since the motorman's cab is on the right-hand side, caution signals should be secured to   24.____
the

    A. right-hand running rail
    B. left-hand running rail
    C. structure to the right of the track
    D. structure to the left of the track

25. In a track work gang, the person responsible for the proper display of signals is the   25.____

    A. track worker   B. foreman
    C. motorman   D. flagman

KEY (CORRECT ANSWERS)

1.	D		11.	C
2.	B		12.	B
3.	C		13.	A
4.	A		14.	D
5.	C		15.	B
6.	C		16.	C
7.	C		17.	B
8.	A		18.	B
9.	D		19.	C
10.	A		20.	D

21.	D
22.	A
23.	D
24.	C
25.	B

TEST 3

DIRECTIONS: Each question or incomplete statement is followed by several suggested answers or completions. Select the one that BEST answers the question or completes the statement. *PRINT THE LETTER OF THE CORRECT ANSWER IN THE SPACE AT THE RIGHT.*

Questions 1-6.

DIRECTIONS: Questions 1 through 6 are to be answered on the basis of the Bulletin Order given below. Refer to this bulletin when answering these questions.

BULLETIN ORDER NO. 67

SUBJECT: Procedure for Handling Fire Occurrences

   In order that the Fire Department may be notified of all fires, even those that have been extinguished by our own employees, any employee having knowledge of a fire must notify the Station Department Office immediately on telephone extensions D-4177, D-4181, D-4185, or D-4189.

   Specific information regarding the fire should include the location of the fire, the approximate distance north or south of the nearest station, and the track designation, line, and division.

   In addition, the report should contain information as to the status of the fire and whether our forces have extinguished it or if Fire Department equipment is required.

   When all information has been obtained, the Station Supervisor in Charge in the Station Department Office will notify the Desk Trainmaster of the Division involved.

Richard Roe,
Superintendent

1. An employee having knowledge of a fire should FIRST notify the   1.____

    A.   Station Department Office
    B.   Fire Department
    C.   Desk Trainmaster
    D.   Station Supervisor

2. If bulletin order number 1 was issued on January 2, bulletins are being issued at the   2.____
    monthly average of

    A.   8   B.   10   C.   12   D.   14

3. It is clear from the bulletin that   3.____

    A.   employees are expected to be expert fire fighters
    B.   many fires occur on the transit system
    C.   train service is usually suspended whenever a fire occurs
    D.   some fires are extinguished without the help of the Fire Department

4. From the information furnished in this bulletin, it can be assumed that the   4.____

    A. Station Department office handles a considerable number of telephone calls
    B. Superintendent Investigates the handling of all subway fires
    C. Fire Department is notified only in ease of large fires
    D. employee first having knowledge of the fire must call all 4 extensions

5. The PROBABLE reason for notifying the Fire Department even when the fire has been   5.____
extinguished by a subway employee is because the Fire Department is

    A. a city agency
    B. still responsible to check the fire
    C. concerned with fire prevention
    D. required to clean up after the fire

6. Information about the fire NOT specifically required is   6.____

    A. track   B. time of day   C. station   D. division

Questions 7-10.

DIRECTIONS: Questions 7 through 10 are to be answered on the basis of the paragraph on
fire fighting shown below. When answering these questions, refer to this paragraph.

FIRE FIGHTING

A security officer should remember the cardinal rule that water or soda acid fire extin-
guishers should not be used on any electrical fire, and apply it in the case of a fire near the
third rail. In addition, security officers should familiarize themselves with all available fire
alarms and fire-fighting equipment within their assigned posts. Use of the fire alarm should
bring responding Fire Department apparatus quickly to the scene. Familiarity with the fire-
fighting equipment near his post would help in putting out incipient fires. Any man calling for
the Fire Department should remain outside so that he can direct the Fire Department to the
fire. As soon as possible thereafter, the special inspection desk must be notified, and a complete written report of the fire, no matter how small, must be submitted to this office. The
security officer must give the exact time and place it started, who discovered it, how it was
extinguished, the damage done, cause of same, list of any injured persons with the extent of
their injuries, and the name of the Fire Chief in charge. All defects noticed by the security
officer concerning the fire alarm or any fire-fighting equipment must be reported to the special
inspection department.

7. It would be PROPER to use water to put out a fire in a(n)   7.____

    A. electric motor   B. electric switch box
    C. waste paper trash can   D. electric generator

8. After calling the Fire Department from a street box to report a fire, the security officer   8.____
should then

    A. return to the fire and help put it out
    B. stay outside and direct the Fire Department to the fire
    C. find a phone and call his boss
    D. write out a report for the special inspection desk

9. A security officer is required to submit a complete written report of a fire   9._____

    A. two weeks after the fire
    B. the day following the fire
    C. as soon as possible
    D. at his convenience

10. In his report of a fire, it is NOT necessary for the security officer to state   10._____

    A. time and place of the fire
    B. who discovered the fire
    C. the names of persons injured
    D. quantity of Fire Department equipment used

Questions 11-16.

DIRECTIONS: Questions 11 through 16 are to be answered on the basis of the Notice given
              below. Refer to this Notice in answering these questions.

NOTICE

Your attention is called to Route Request Buttons that are installed on all new type Interlocking Home Signals where there is a choice of route in the midtown area. The route request
button is to be operated by the motorman when the home signal is at danger and no call-on is
displayed or when improper route is displayed.

To operate, the motorman will press the button for the desiredroute as indicated under
each button; a light will then go on over the buttons to inform the motorman that his request
has been registered in the tower.

If the towerman desires to give the motorman a route other than the one he selected, the
towerman will cancel out the light over the route selection buttons. The motorman will then
accept the route given.

If no route or call-on is given, the motorman will sound his whistle for the signal maintainer, secure his train, and call the desk trainmaster.

11. The official titles of the two classes of employee whose actions would MOST frequently   11._____
     be affected by the contents of this notice are

    A. motorman and trainmaster
    B. signal maintainer and trainmaster
    C. towerman and motorman
    D. signal maintainer and towerman

12. A motorman should use a route request button when   12._____

    A. the signal indicates proceed on main line
    B. a call-on is displayed
    C. the signal indicates stop
    D. the signal indicates proceed on diverging route

13. The PROPER way to request a route is to   13._____

    A. press the button corresponding to the desired route
    B. press the button a number of times to correspond with the number of the route requested
    C. stop at the signal and blow four short blasts
    D. stop at the signal and telephone the tower

14. The motorman will know that his requested route has been registered in the tower if   14._____

    A. a light comes on over the route request buttons
    B. an acknowledging signal is sounded on the tower horn
    C. the light in the route request button goes dark
    D. the home signal continues to indicate stop

15. Under certain conditions, when stopped at such home signal, the motorman must signal   15._____
for a signal maintainer and call the desk trainmaster.
Such condition exists when, after standing awhile,

    A. the towerman continues to give the wrong route
    B. the towerman does not acknowledge the signal
    C. no route or call-on is given
    D. the light over the route request buttons is cancelled out

16. It is clear that route request buttons   16._____

    A. eliminate train delays due to signals at junctions
    B. keep the towerman alert
    C. force motormen and towermen to be more careful
    D. are a more accurate form of communication than the whistle.

Questions 17-22.

DIRECTIONS: Questions 17 through 22 are to be answered on the basis of the instructions for removal of paper given below. Read these instructions carefully before answering these questions.

GENERAL INSTRUCTIONS FOR REMOVAL OF PAPER

    When a cleaner's work schedule calls for the bagging of paper, he will remove paper from the waste paper receptacles, bag it, and place the bags at the head end of the platform, where they will be picked up by the work train. He will fill bags with paper to a weight that can be carried without danger of personal injury, as porters are forbidden to drag bags of paper over the platform. Cleaners are responsible that all bags of paper are arranged so as to prevent their falling from the platform to tracks, and so as to not interfere with passenger traffic.

17. A GOOD reason for removing the paper from receptacles and placing it in bags is that   17._____
bags are more easily

    A. stored   B. weighed   C. handled   D. emptied

18. The *head end* of a local station platform is the end

    A. in the direction that trains are running
    B. nearest to which the trains stop
    C. where there is an underpass to the other side
    D. at which the change booth is located

18.____

19. The MOST likely reason for having the filled bags placed at the head end of the station rather than at the other end is that

    A. a special storage space is provided there for them
    B. this end of the platform is farthest from the passengers
    C. most porters' closets are located near the head end
    D. the work train stops at this end to pick them up

19.____

20. Limiting the weight to which the bags can be filled is PROBABLY done to

    A. avoid having too many ripped or broken bags
    B. protect the porter against possible rupture
    C. make sure that all bags are filled fairly evenly
    D. insure that, when stored, the bags will not fall to the track

20.____

21. The MOST important reason for not allowing filled bags to be dragged over the platform is that the bags

    A. could otherwise be loaded too heavily
    B. might leave streaks on the platform
    C. would wear out too quickly
    D. might spill paper on the platform

21.____

22. The instructions do NOT hold a porter responsible for a bag of paper which

    A. is torn due to dragging over a platform
    B. falls on a passenger because it was poorly stacked
    C. falls to the track without being pushed
    D. is ripped open by school children

22.____

Questions 23-25.

DIRECTIONS: Questions 23 through 25 are to be answered on the basis of the situation described below. Consider the facts given in this situation when answering these questions.

SITUATION

A new detergent that is to be added to water and the resulting mixture just wiped on any surface has been tested by the station department and appeared to be excellent. However, you notice, after inspecting a large number of stations that your porters have cleaned with this detergent, that the surfaces cleaned are not as clean as they formerly were when the old method was used.

23. The MAIN reason for the station department testing the new detergent in the first place was to make certain that

    A. it was very simple to use
    B. a little bit would go a long way
    C. there was no stronger detergent on the market
    D. it was superior to anything formerly used

23.____

24. The MAIN reason that such a poor cleaning job resulted was MOST likely due to the

    A. porters being lax on the job
    B. detergent not being as good as expected
    C. incorrect amount of water being mixed with the detergent
    D. fact that the surfaces cleaned needed to be scrubbed

24.____

25. The reason for inspecting a number of stations was to

    A. determine whether all porters did the same job
    B. insure that the result of the cleaning job was the same in each location
    C. be certain that the detergent was used in each station inspected
    D. see whether certain surfaces cleaned better than others

25.____

KEY (CORRECT ANSWERS)

1.	A		11.	C
2.	C		12.	C
3.	D		13.	A
4.	A		14.	A
5.	C		15.	C
6.	B		16.	D
7.	C		17.	C
8.	B		18.	A
9.	C		19.	D
10.	D		20.	B

21.	C
22.	D
23.	D
24.	B
25.	B

ARITHMETICAL REASONING

EXAMINATION SECTION
TEST 1

DIRECTIONS: Each question or incomplete statement is followed by several suggested answers or completions. Select the one that BEST answers the question or completes the statement. *PRINT THE LETTER OF THE CORRECT ANSWER IN THE SPACE AT THE RIGHT.*

1. The distance covered in four minutes by a subway train traveling at 30 mph is _____ mile(s).   1.____

    A. 1   B. 1 1/2   C. 2   D. 3

2. The jaws of a vise close 3/16" for each turn of the screw. If the vise is open 6 inches, the number of turns to close the jaws completely is   2.____

    A. 29   B. 30   C. 31   D. 32

3. The sum of 3"2 1/4", 0'8 7/8", 2'9 3/4", and 1'0" is   3.____

    A. 7'8 7/8"   B. 7'9"
    C. 8'0 7/8"   D. 15'0 7/8"

4. It was estimated that a certain track concreting job would require 40 cubic yards of concrete. Actually, the job took 38 1/2 cubic yards.
The percentage error from the estimate is MOST NEARLY   4.____

    A. 2%   B. 4%   C. 6%   D. 8%

5. A 39-foot length of running rail weighing 100 lbs. per yard has a total weight of _____ lbs.   5.____

    A. 390   B. 780   C. 1,300   D. 3,900

6. The pay of a trackman for a 40-hour week at $19.39 an hour is   6.____

    A. $775.60   B. $738.60   C. $777.60   D. $789.60

7. If a train on a certain route makes two roundtrips in 5 hours and 20 minutes, the average time for one roundtrip would be _____ hour(s) _____ minutes.   7.____

    A. 1; 20   B. 2; 30   C. 2; 40   D. 3; 10

8. It is estimated that it will take 6 men working for 6 days to complete a certain track maintenance job.
If, when the job is started, only 4 men can be made available, you can estimate that the number of days needed for these men to complete the job will be   8.____

    A. 4   B. 6   C. 9   D. 13 1/2

9. A certain track job, which takes 3 days to complete, requires 7 trackmen at $16.245 per hour and a gang foreman whose annual salary is equivalent to $138.60 per day.
The TOTAL labor cost for the job is (assuming an 8-hr. work day)   9.____

    A. $756.91   B. $1,325.52   C. $3,144.96   D. $8,671.20

10. A certain track job, which took 4 days to complete, required 6 trackmen at $15.15 per hour and a gang foreman whose annual salary is equivalent to $128.00 per day. The TOTAL labor cost for the job was

    A. $855.20   B. $875.60   C. $1,239.20   D. $3,420.80

10.____

11. The sum of the fractions 5/16, 5/8, and 21/32 is MOST NEARLY

    A. 1.491   B. 1.594   C. 1.630   D. 1.642

11.____

12. If a maintainer earns $10.82 per hour and time and one-half for overtime, his gross salary for a week in which he works 2 hours over his regular 40 hours should be

    A. $433.60   B. $449.86   C. $455.28   D. $465.26

12.____

13. It is common knowledge among railroad men that a speed of 15 miles per hour is exactly equal to 22 feet per second.
In accordance with this rule, select the FASTEST of the following speeds:

    A. 70 feet per second   B. 50 miles per hour
    C. 0.9 mile per minute   D. 4,500 feet per minute

13.____

14. Several months ago, the rush hour headway on the Rockaway Line was increased from 16 minutes to 24 minutes.
This represents a reduction in train service of APPROXIMATELY (SEE NOTE BELOW)

    A. 25%   B. 33%   C. 50%   D. 67%

14.____

15. The running time between two local terminals is 40 minutes. If the average speed of the trains on this run is 15 mph, the distance between these terminals is APPROXIMATELY _____ miles.

    A. 8   B. 10   C. 12   D. 14

15.____

16. A ten-car train took 6 minutes to travel between two stations which are 3 miles apart. The average speed of the train was _____ mph.

    A. 20   B. 25   C. 30   D. 35

16.____

17. Trains on a certain track operate on a 2-minute headway at a speed of 30 miles per hour. A CORRECT expression for calculating the number of feet of distance between the front of one train and the front of the train ahead when both trains are running at the given speed is

    A. 30/60 x 2 x 5,280   B. 2/30 x 60 x 5,280
    C. 30/60 x 1/2 x 5,280   D. 30/2 x 1/60 x 5,280

NOTE: Assume headway is calculated by dividing the total number of cars by the time, in minutes, required to pass a particular point.

17.____

18. Motormen are permitted to *economize* on time when it can be done safely after a delay. In order to save one minute on a one-mile stretch for which the timetable schedules an average speed of 15 miles per hour, the motormen would have to average _____ mph.

    A. 17   B. 20   C. 22   D. 25

18.____

19. If the distance between two terminals is 8.3 miles, then a train which made 6 roundtrips traveled about _____ miles.

   A. 50   B. 65   C. 85   D. 100

19.____

20. A certain subway line has been extended to include five more local stations. Assuming that the schedule time for each local run averages 1 1/2 minutes, the number of minutes that should be added to the scheduled roundtrip time due to this extension is NEAREST to _____ minutes.

   A. 7 1/2   B. 10   C. 12 1/2   D. 15

20.____

21. The first of three storage tracks holds as many cars as the other two together, and the second holds twice as many cars as the third.
If the first track holds 30 cars, the first and third tracks together hold _____ cars.

   A. 60   B. 50   C. 45   D. 40

21.____

22. In a four-track lay-up yard, there are 3 cars on each of two tracks and 6 cars on each of the other two tracks. If each lay-up track can hold 10 cars, the MINIMUM number of train movements required to set up a ten-car train on one of the lay-up tracks is

   A. 2   B. 3   C. .4   D. 5

22.____

23. The service on a certain four-track line consists of 24 trains per hour on each express track and 21 trains per hour on each local track. Assume there are 2 locals & 2 express tracks. The TOTAL number of all trains passing a given point on this line in any 10-minute period is

   A. 7   B. 9   C. 15   D. 45

23.____

24. An express train requires five minutes to make the run between two stations which are two miles apart.
The AVERAGE speed of the train, in miles per hour, for this run is

   A. 15   B. 20   C. 24   D. 30

24.____

25. A road motorman, paid $13.40 an hour, reports for work on Wednesday at 7:30 A.M. and normally clears at 3:00 P.M.
What is his gross pay for the day if he is required to take 1 hr. to write an unusual occurrence report at the end of this run?

   A. $105.20   B. $107.20   C. $113.90   D. $120.60

25.____

KEY (CORRECT ANSWERS)

1. C
2. D
3. A
4. B
5. C
6. A
7. C
8. C
9. C
10. D

11. B
12. D
13. C
14. B
15. B
16. C
17. A
18. B
19. D
20. D

21. D
22. A
23. C
24. C
25. C

SOLUTIONS TO PROBLEMS

1. Let x = distance in miles. Then, 30/60=x/4. Solving, x = 2

2. Number of turns = $6 \div \dfrac{3}{16} = 32$

3. 3' 2 1/4" + 0'8 7/8" + 2' 9 3/4" + 1'0" = 6'20 7/8" = 7' 8 7/8"

4. (40-38 1/2) ÷ 40 = 3.75% ≈ 4%

5. (100)(39/3) = 1300 lbs.

6. ($19.39)(40) = $775.60

7. (5 hrs. 20 min.) ÷ 2 = 320 min. ÷ 2 = 160 min. = 2 hrs. 40 min.

8. (6)(6) = 36 man-days. Then, 36 ÷ 4 = 9 days

9. Total cost = (8)(3)(7)($16.245) + (3)($138.60) = $3144.96

10. Total cost = (4)(6)($15.15)(8) + (4)($128.00) = $3420.80

11. 5/16 + 4/8 + 21/32=1.59375 ≈ 1-594

12. ($10.82)(40) + ($16.23)(2) = $465.26

13. A: 70 ft/sec = (70/22)(15) = 47.73 mph; B: 50 mph; C: .9 mi/min. =44 (.9)(60) = 54 mph; D: 4500 ft/min = 75 ft/sec = (75/22)(15) ~ 51.14 mph So, C is fastest.

14. (24-16) ÷ 24 = 1/3 ≈ 33%

15. Let x = miles. Then, 15/60=x/40. Solving, x = 10

16. (3)(60/6) = 30 mph

17. Distance = 30/60 x 2 x 5280 = 5280 ft.

18. 15 mph = 1 mi. in 4 min. If this 1 mi. is reduced to 3 min., then rate = 60/3 = 20 mph

19. (8.3)(12) = 99.6 ≈ 100 miles. Note: 1 roundtrip = 16.6 miles

20. (5)(2)(1 1/2) = 15 min.

21. Let x, 2x = number of cars for the 3rd and 2nd tracks, respectively. Then, x + 2x = 30, so x = 10. Since the 1st track holds 30 cars, the 1st and 3rd tracks hold 40 cars.

22. 2 movements are required. Move the 3 cars on each track containing 3 cars over to the track (other one) containing 6 cars. However, from one of the tracks containing 3 cars, just move 1 car to the 6-car track (6+3+1 =10)

23. [(24)(2)+(21)(2)] ÷ 6 = 15 trains in a 10-minute period. We assume there are 2 local tracks and 2 express tracks.

24. Let x = mph. Then, 2/5 = x/60. Solving, x = 24

25. ($13.40)(8.5) = $113.90

TEST 2

DIRECTIONS: Each question or incomplete statement is followed by several suggested answers or completions. Select the one that BEST answers the question or completes the statement. *PRINT THE LETTER OF THE CORRECT ANSWER IN THE SPACE AT THE RIGHT.*

1. A trainmaster standing on a local station times the passing of an express train as 16 seconds.
   If the express was 610 feet long, its AVERAGE speed passing the trainmaster was _____ mph.

   A. 24   B. 26   C. 28   D. 30

   1.____

2. A trainmaster stations himself opposite the head end of a 440-foot-long local train which has stopped in the station. This train takes 28 seconds to pass the trainmaster after it has started.
   Considering that this is an actual rather than a theoretical train, the rear of the train passes the trainmaster at a speed which is CLOSEST to _____ mph.

   A. 10   B. 14   C. 18   D. 22

   2.____

3. A 12 1/2 percent increase on a $1.40 fare would be MOST closely approximated by charging fares at

   A. 5 for $7.87   B. 6 for $7.84
   C. 8 for $8.60   D. 10 for $16.80

   3.____

4. A special fare operation will require that 3 motormen, 4 conductors, and 2 towermen be assigned to this service on an 8-hour basis each day that the operation is in effect. Assuming that all other operating costs come to 25% of the wages of the personnel already specified, the MINIMUM number of daily passengers to just cover costs at a 40-cent fare would have to be

   A. 420   B. 540   C. 680   D. 800

   4.____

5. If a speed of 15 miles per hour is exactly 22 feet per second, then the number of miles per hour corresponding to 40 feet per second is MOST NEARLY

   A. 10   B. 20   C. 25   D. 30

   5.____

6. If the average speed of a train is 20 mph, the time it takes the train to travel 1 mile is minutes.

   A. 2   B. 3   C. 4   D. 5

   6.____

7. If the average speed of a train between two stations is 30 miles per hour, and the two stations are 1/2 mile apart, the time it takes the train to travel from one station to the other is _____ minute(s).

   A. 1   B. 2   C. 3   D. 4

   7.____

8. A lay-up yard has five equal length tracks that can hold a total of 55 cars.
   If 8 cars are laid up on one track and six cars on each of the other four, the additional number of cars that can be laid up in this yard is

   A. 8   B. 23   C. 24   D. 32

   8.____

9. If twelve 10-car trains and eight 8-car trains pass a point on a certain track during one hour, the headway on that track is _____ minutes.

    A. 6   B. 5   C. 4   D. 3

9._____

10. The running time of a train between two terminals is 48 minutes, and there is a 7-minute layover at each terminal. If a train leaves one terminal at 11:00 A.M., this train is due back at the same terminal at

    A. 11:48 A.M.   B. 11:55 A.M.
    C. 12:43 P.M.   D. 12:50 P.M.

10._____

11. A motorman's weekly pay for 8 hours a day, 5 days a week, at $13.32 an hour is

    A. $533.20   B. $532.80   C. $528.80   D. $493.20

11._____

12. If seven 10-car trains and eight 8-car trains pass a point on a certain track during one hour, the headway on that track is _____ minutes. (Refer to note on page 2/Test 1.)

    A. 2   B. 4   C. 5   D. 6

12._____

13. If the average speed of a train is 30 miles per hour, the time it takes the train to travel one mile is_____ minutes.

    A. 2   B. 3   C. 4   D. 5

13._____

14. A 5-track lay-up yard can hold a total of 5 ten-car trains. There are already 5 cars stored on each of 4 tracks and 10 cars stored on the fifth track.
The number of additional cars that can be stored in this yard is

    A. 20   B. 25   C. 30   D. 32

14._____

15. If a train takes 4 minutes to travel between 2 stations that are 1 mile apart, the average speed of the train is APPROXIMATELY_____ mph.

    A. 5   B. 15   C. 25   D. 35

15._____

16. A seven-track lay-up yard can hold 16 cars on each track, but there are already five 8-car trains in this yard.
The number of additional cars that can be stored in this yard is

    A. 40   B. 60   C. 72   D. 112

16._____

17. A motorman's weekly pay for 8 hours a day, 5 days a week, at $13.50 an hour is

    A. $108.00   B. $480.00   C. $540.00   D. $555.00

17._____

18. A train moving at the rate of 24 miles per hour will travel 4 miles in_____ minutes.

    A. 6   B. 10   C. 20   D. 96

18._____

19. If a certain motorman earns $472.00 each week and works 40 hours each week, his rate of pay per hour is

    A. $11.50   B. $11.60   C. $11.70   D. $11.80

19._____

20. A train moving at the rate of 30 miles per hour will travel 6 miles in _____ minutes.

    A. 5   B. 8   C. 10   D. 12

20._____

21. A certain motorman reports for work at 8 A.M. on Tuesday and normally clears at 3:30   21.____
P.M. He is paid at the hourly rate of $11.80.
What should his gross pay be for this day if, due to a train delay, he gets only 10 minutes for lunch?

    A. $94.40   B. $100.30   C. $104.20   D. $106.20

22. A certain towerman reports for work at 8 A.M. on Tuesday and normally clears at 3:30   22.____
P.M. He is paid at the hourly rate of $12.40. If it takes an hour to write a report, what is his gross pay for this day if he is required to write an unusual occurrence report at the end of his run?

    A. $99.20   B. $105.40   C. $110.40   D. $117.40

23. A motorman reports for work at 7 A.M. on Tuesday and normally clears at 2:30 P.M. He is   23.____
paid at the hourly rate of $12.80.
What is his gross pay for this day if he has a student motorman with him for an extra 2 1/2 hours?

    A. $102.40   B. $115.20   C. $128.00   D. $140.00

24. A certain conductor reports at 8 A.M. and normally clears at 3 P.M. His hourly rate of pay   24.____
is $11.00.
What should his gross pay be for this day if he is late at the end of his run and clears at 4 P.M.?

    A. $88.00   B. $92.50   C. $99.00   D. $102.50

25. The speed of a train that travels 6 miles in 12 minutes is_____ mph.   25.____

    A. 20   B. 30   C. 40   D. 50

————

KEY (CORRECT ANSWERS)

1. B	11. B
2. D	12. A
3. A	13. A
4. C	14. A
5. C	15. B
6. B	16. C
7. A	17. C
8. B	18. B
9. D	19. D
10. C	20. D

21. B
22. B
23. C
24. A
25. B

SOLUTIONS TO PROBLEMS

1. 610' in 16 sec. = (610')(225) = 137,250' in 1 hour. Then, 137,250 ÷ 5280 ≈ 26 mph

2. 440' in 28 sec. ≈ (440')(128.57) ≈ 56,571' in 1 hour. Then, 56,571 ÷ 5280 ≈ 11 mph average speed. Thus, the final speed can be found by solving for x: (0+x)/2 = 11. Solving, x = 22

3. ($1.40)(1.125) = $1.575. This is closest to 5 for $7.84, which is $1.568 apiece.

4. Can't be done. Insufficient information

5. (15)(40/22) = 27.27 mph, closest to 25 mph

6. 60/20 = 3min.

7. 30 nph means 1 min. to travel 1/2 mile

8. 55 - 8 - (6)(4) = 23 additional cars

9. (12)(10) + (8)(8) = 184. Then, 184 ÷ 60 ≈ 3 min.

10. 11:00 AM + 48 min. + 7 min. + 48 min. = 12:43 PM

11. (8)(5)($13.32) = $532.80

12. (7)(10) + (8)(8) = 134. Then, 134 ÷ 60 ≈ 2 min.

13. Let x = number of minutes. Then, 30/60 = 1/x . Solving, x = 2

14. 50 - (5)(4) - 10 = 20 additional cars

15. Let x = average speed in mph. Then, x/60 = 1/4. Solving, x = 15

16. (16)(7) - (5)(8) = 72 additional cars

17. (8)(5)($13.50) = $540.00

18. Let x = number of minutes. Then, 24/60=4/x . Solving, x = 10

19. $472.00 ÷ 40 = $11.80 per hour

20. Let x = number of minutes. Then, 30/60 = 6/x . Solving, x = 12

21. ($11.80)(8.5) = $100.30

22. ($12.40)(8.5) = $105.40

23. ($12.80X10) = $128.00

24. ($11.00)(8) = $88.00

25. Let x = speed in mph. Then, 6/12=x/60. Solving, x = 30

TEST 3

DIRECTIONS: Each question or incomplete statement is followed by several suggested answers or completions. Select the one that BEST answers the question or completes the statement. *PRINT THE LETTER OF THE CORRECT ANSWER IN THE SPACE AT THE RIGHT.*

1. A certain subway train on straight level track has an acceleration rate of 1.7 miles per hour per second up to 18 mph.
   The distance this train must travel on straight level track to accelerate from 8 mph to 18 mph is about _____ feet.

   A. 75   B. 95   C. 110   D. 140   1.____

2. The average service braking rate of the R-10 and later subway cars is 2.5 miles per hour per second whereas on earlier cars the service braking rate average 1.5 miles per hour per second.
   The number of seconds saved by the use of the newer equipment in service braking from 26 miles per hour to a stop is approximately

   A. 17.3   B. 10.4   C. 6.9   D. 3.5   2.____

3. Ninety percent of the 240 conductors and motormen reporting daily at a certain terminal are married, and 40% of all conductors and motormen are under 35 years of age.
   The MINIMUM number of married conductors and motormen in this lower age group is

   A. 48   B. 60   C. 72   D. 84   3.____

4. If a train having a length of 600 feet passes a point in 10 seconds, its speed, in miles per hour, is CLOSEST to

   A. 39   B. 41   C. 86   D. 88   4.____

5. A train is 450 feet long and travels at a rate of 45 mph. The length of time it takes this train to pass a certain point is CLOSEST to _____ seconds.

   A. 6.8   B. 7.0   C. 14.5   D. 14.7   5.____

6. The running time from terminal to terminal for a certain line is 50 minutes, and the relay time is 6 minutes at each terminal.
   How many additional cars are required to increase the present eight-car service to ten cars while maintaining the present headway of 8 minutes?

   A. 24   B. 26   C. 28   D. 30   6.____

7. The length of a train which passes a certain point in 15 seconds while moving at a speed of 20 mph is _____ feet.

   A. 204   B. 210   C. 440   D. 450   7.____

8. The average speed of a train between two terminals 6 miles apart is 12 mph.
   The time required to make one roundtrip allowing 15 minutes for relay time at the far terminal is ____ minutes.

   A. 60   B. 65   C. 70   D. 75   8.____

9. Each track of a four track lay-up yard can hold 10 cars. There are a total of 10 cars   9.____
   already in this yard.
   The number of additional cars that can be stored in this yard is

   A. 35   B. 30   C. 25   D. 20

10. What is the speed of a train that travels five miles in ten minutes?   10.____
    _____ mph.

   A. 24   B. 25   C. 28   D. 30

11. If a certain conductor earns $360.00 a week and works 40 hours, his salary per hour is   11.____

   A. $10.00   B. $8.50   C. $9.00   D. $9.50

12. A conductor earns $10.82 per hour. He is paid time and one-half for each hour worked   12.____
    over 40 hours per week. If a conductor works 44 hours in one week, his gross salary for
    that week is

   A. $497.68   B. $497.72   C. $499.72   D. $499.92

13. An 8-car subway train consisting of 75-foot cars took 60 seconds to enter and clear a   13.____
    620-foot station without stopping.
    The speed of this train was MOST NEARLY _____ mph.

   A. 7   B. 14   C. 18   D. 28

14. A certain motorman reports at 8:00 A.M. and normally clears at 3:30 P.M. His hourly rate   14.____
    of pay is $12.40. What should his gross pay be for this day if he is late at the end of his
    run and clears at 4:30 P.M.?

   A. $105.40   B. $111.60   C. $114.00   D. $117.80

15. The FASTEST of the following speeds is   15.____

   A. 85 feet per second   B. 0.95 mile per minute
   C. 57 miles per hour   D. 5,000 feet per minute

16. An eight-car train leaves a terminal carrying in each car, respectively, passenger loads of   16.____
    173, 182, 147, 152, 145, 148, 180, and 170.
    Using a capacity of 210 passengers per car, the AVERAGE passenger loading per car
    is about

   A. 70%   B. 77%   C. 80%   D. 85%

17. For certain cars, the service braking distance is about 40% greater when fully loaded   17.____
    than when empty.
    If the fully loaded service braking distance from 35 mph is 465 feet, the service braking
    distance for empty cars under the same conditions should be about _____ feet.

   A. 185   B. 280   C. 330   D. 650

18. A special fare operation requires that 4 motormen, 6 conductors, and 2 towermen be assigned to the service. The men start at 8:00 A.M. and clear at 3:45 P.M. The rate of pay for a motorman is $18 per hour, for a conductor $16 per hour, and for a towerman $17.60 per hour. The 12 men have no other assignments.
Assuming that all other operating costs come to 25% of the wages of the personnel already specified, the MINIMUM number of daily passengers to just cover cost at $3.00 fare would have to be NEAREST to

    A. 600   B. 660   C. 720   D. 770

18.____

19. The roundtrip time between two terminals, not including layover time, is 1 hour, 20 minutes.
A train due to arrive at one terminal at 9:10 should leave the other terminal at

    A. 7:50   B. 8:00   C. 8:10   D. 8:30

19.____

20. An express train requires five minutes to make the run between two stations which are two and one-half miles apart.
The AVERAGE speed of the train for this run is ____ mph.

    A. 24   B. 30   C. 36   D. 42

20.____

21. If twenty 10-car trains and ten 8-car trains pass a point on a certain track during one hour, the headway on that track, in minutes, is (See note in Test 1,question 12.)

    A. 1 1/2   B. 2   C. 3   D. 5

21.____

22. If the average speed of a train is 30 miles per hour, the time it takes the train to travel one mile is ____ minute(s).

    A. 1   B. 2   C. 3   D. 4

22.____

23. A 5-track lay-up yard can hold a total of 5 ten-car trains. There are already 3 cars stored on each of 4 tracks and 4 cars stored on the fifth track.
The number of additional cars that can be stored in this yard is

    A. 14   B. 24   C. 34   D. 44

23.____

24. A six-track lay-up yard can hold 12 cars on each track but there are already four 10-car trains in this yard.
The number of additional cars that can be stored in this yard is

    A. 12   B. 32   C. 40   D. 72

24.____

25. An express train requires five minutes to make the run between two stations which are two miles apart.
The AVERAGE speed of the train, in miles per hour, for this run is

    A. 20   B. 24   C. 30   D. 36

25.____

KEY (CORRECT ANSWERS)

1. C
2. C
3. C
4. B
5. A

6. C
7. C
8. D
9. B
10. D

11. C
12. B
13. B
14. A
15. A

16. B
17. C
18. B
19. D
20. B

21. D
22. B
23. C
24. B
25. B

SOLUTIONS TO PROBLEMS

1. 8 mph = 11.7$\overline{3}$ ft/sec, 1.7 m/hr/sec = 2.49$\overline{3}$ ft/sec^2. The formula for distance is d = vt + 1/2gt^2 , where v = the initial velocity, g = rate of acceleration, and t = time. To determine time, t = (18-8.) $\div$ 1.7 $\approx$ 5.88 sec. Thus, d = (11.73)(5.88) + (1/2)(2.49$\overline{3}$)(5.88^2) $\approx$ 112 ft., closest to 110 ft,

2. For the R-10, the time = (26-0) $\div$ 2.5 = 10.4 *sec.*, whereas the time for the earlier cars = (26-0) $\div$ 1.5 = 17.$\overline{3}$ sec. The time saved is approximately 6.9 sec. (Actual time = 6.9$\overline{3}$ sec)

3. Let x = number of individuals both married and under 35 years old. Then, the number of individuals married but NOT under 35 years old = (.90)(240) - x = 216 - x. Likewise, the number of individuals under 35 years old but not married = (.40)(240) - x = 96 - x. Thus, (216-x) + x + (96-x) $\leq$ 240. Solving, x $\geq$ 72

4. Let x = speed in mph. Then, 600/10 = y/3600. Thus, y = 216,000 ft/hr. To find x, divide y by 5280. So, x $\approx$ 41

5. 45 mph = 66 ft/sec. Then, 450 $\div$ 66 $\approx$ 6.8 sec.

6. Unable to solve

7. 20 mph = 29 1/3 ft/sec. Then, (29 1/3) (15) = 440 ft.

8. At 12 mph, 6 miles can be traveled in 1/2 hour (or 30 minutes). Then, 30 + 15 + 30 = 75 minutes.

9. (10)(4) - 10 = 30 additional cars

10. 5 miles in 10 minutes = (5)(6) = 30 mph

11. $360.00 $\div$ 40 = $9.00 per hour

12. ($10.82)(40) + ($16.23)(4) = $497.72

13. (8)(75) = 600 ft. The train went 600 + 620 = 1220 ft. in 1 minute. This is equivalent to 73,200 ft. per hour. Finally, 73,200 $\div$ 5280 $\approx$ 14 mph.

14. (8.5)($12.40) = $105.40

15. A: 85 ft/sec = (85/88)(60) $\approx$ 57.95 mph; B: .95 mi/min = (.95)(60) = 57 mph; C: As is 57 mph; D: 5000 ft/min = 83.$\overline{3}$ ft/sec = (83$\overline{3}$/88) (60) $\approx$ 56-82 mph. Thus, A is fastest.

16. (173+182+147+152+145+148+180+170) $\div$ 8 = 162.125 Then, 162.125 $\div$ 210 $\approx$ 77%

17. 465 $\div$ 1.40 $\approx$ 332 ft., closest to 330 ft.

18. (4)(7.75)($18) + (6)(7.75)($16) + (2)(7.75)($17.60) = $1574.80.
Now, (1.25)(1574.80) = 1,968.50.
Finally, $1,968.50 $\div$ $3.00 = 656.16, closest to 660 passengers.

19. (1 hr. 20 min.) ÷ 2 = 40 minutes. Then, 9:10 - 40 min. = 8:30

20. 2 1/2 miles in 5 minutes = (2 1/2)(12) = 30 mph

21. [(20)(10)+(10)(8)] ÷ 60 = 4 2/3 ≈ 5 min.

22. 30 mph = 60/30 = 2 min, to travel 1 mile

23. (5)(10) - (3)(4) - (4)(1) = 34 additional cars

24. (6)(12) - (4)(10) = 32 additional cars

25. 2 miles in 5 minutes means (2)(60/5) = 24 mph

———

INTERPRETING STATISTICAL DATA
GRAPHS, CHARTS AND TABLES

EXAMINATION SECTION
TEST 1

DIRECTIONS: Each question or incomplete statement is followed by several suggested answers or completions. Select the one that BEST answers the question or completes the statement. *PRINT THE LETTER OF THE CORRECT ANSWER IN THE SPACE AT THE RIGHT.*

Questions 1-9.

DIRECTIONS: Questions 1 through 9 are to be answered SOLELY on the basis of the bus timetable shown below. Assume layover time at Prince St. and Duke St. is negligible.

	EASTBOUND					WESTBOUND		
	King St.	Prince St.	Duke St.	Queen St.		Duke St.	Prince St.	King St.
Bus No.	Lv.	Lv.	Lv.	Arr.	Lv.	Lv.	Lv.	Arr.
20	7:15	7:20	7:30	7:45	7:50	8:05	8:15	8:20
21	7:25	7:30	7:40	7:55	8:00	8:15	8:25	8:30
22	7:35	7:40	7:50	8:05	8:10	8:25	8:35	8:40
23	7:45	7:50	8:00	8:15	8:20	8:35	8:45	8:50
24	7:55	8:00	8:10	8:25	8:30	8:45	8:55	9:00
25	8:05	8:10	8:20	8:35	8:40	8:55	9:05	9:10
26	8:10	8:15	8:25	8:40	8:43	8:58	9:08	9:13
27	8:15	8:20	8:30	8:45	8:48	9:03	9:13	9:18
28	8:20	8:25	8:35	8:50	8:53	9:08	9:18	9:23
20	8:30	8:35	8:45	9:00	9:05	9:20	9:30	9:35
21	8:40	8:45	8:55	9:10	9:15	9:30	9:40	9:45
22	8:50	8:55	9:05	9:20	9:25	9:40	9: 50	9:55

TIMETABLE - REGENT PARKWAY LINE - WEEKDAYS

1. The TOTAL running time (omit layover) for one roundtrip from King St. to Queen St. and back again is _____ minutes.

   A. 70   B. 65   C. 60   D. 30

2. The LEAST time that any bus stops over at Queen St. is _____ minutes.

   A. 3   B. 5   C. 10   D. 15

1.____

2.____

3. The time required for a bus to make the Eastbound run from King St. to Queen St. is _____ minutes.

    A. 65   B. 60   C. 35   D. 30

3.____

4. The TOTAL number of different buses shown in the timetable is

    A. 8   B. 9   C. 10   D. 12

4.____

5. The timetable shows that the total number of buses which make two roundtrips is

    A. 1   B. 2   C. 3   D. 4

5.____

6. A person reaching Duke St. at 8:28 to leave on a Westbound bus will have to wait _____ minutes.

    A. 2   B. 5   C. 7   D. 10

6.____

7. The SHORTEST running time between any two bus stops is _____ minutes.

    A. 3   B. 5   C. 10   D. 15

7.____

8. The bus which arrives at King St. three minutes after the preceding bus is Bus No.

    A. 20   B. 22   C. 26   D. 28

8.____

9. Bus No. 21 is scheduled to start its second roundtrip from King St. at

    A. 9:45   B. 8:40   C. 8:30   D. 7:25

9.____

KEY (CORRECT ANSWERS)

1. C		6. C	
2. A		7. B	
3. D		8. C	
4. B		9. B	
5. C			

TEST 2

Questions 1-10.

DIRECTIONS: Questions 1 through 10 are to be answered SOLELY on the basis of the DAILY TRAIN SCHEDULE given below.

DAILY TRAIN SCHEDULE RR LOCAL										
SOUTHBOUND							NORTHBOUND			
Wall St.		Ann St.	Deer St.	Bay St.	Ellen St.		Bay St.	Deer St.	Ann St.	Wall St.
Arr .	Lv.	Lv.	Lv.	Lv.	Arr .	Lv.	Lv.	Lv.	Lv.	Arr.
6:00	6:12	6:20	6:24	6:30	6:32	6:42	6:44	6:50	6:54	7:02L
6:10	6:22	6:30	6:34	6:40	6:42	6:52	6:54	7:00	7:04	7:12
6:20	6:32	6:40	6:44	6:50	6:52	7:02	7:04	7:10	7:14	7:22
6:30	6:42	6:50	6:54	7:00	7:02	7:12	7:14	7:20	7:24	7:32L
6:40	6:52	7:00	7:04	7:10	7:12	7:22	7:24	7:30	7:34	7:42
P	7:02	7:10	7:14	7:20	7:22	7:32	7:34	7:40	7:44	7:52
P	7:10	7:18	7:22	7:28	7:30	7:40	7:42	7:48	7:52	8:00
7:12	7:18	7:26	7:30	7:36	7:38	7:48	7:50	7:56	8:00	8:08
7:22	7:26	7:34	7:38	7:44	7:46	7:56	7:58	8:04	8:08	8:16
P	7:34	7:42	7:46	7:52	7:54	8:04	8:06	8:12	8:16	8:24
P	7:40	7:48	7:52	7:58	8:00	8:10	8:12	8:18	8:22	8:30
7:42	7:46	7:54	7:58	8:04	8:06L					

1. Between 7:00 and 7:38, the TOTAL number of trains placed in service at Wall St. is

    A. 1   B. 2   C. 3   D. 4

2. The number of trains which are taken out of service at Wall St. between 7:10 and 8:06 is

    A. 0   B. 1   C. 2   D. 3

3. Between 7:30 and 7:54, the length of time spent by each train at Ellen St. is _____ minutes.

    A. 2   B. 6   C. 8   D. 10

4. The headway leaving Ann St. in the southbound direction after the time of 7:42 is _____ minutes.

    A. 4   B. 6   C. 8   D. 10

5. The TOTAL number of roundtrips between Wall St.. and Ellen St. during the period shown on the schedule is

    A. 9   B. 10   C. 11   D. 12

1.____

2.____

3.____

4.____

5.____

6. The train arriving at Ellen St. at 7:38 is followed by the train which leaves Wall St. at   6._____

    A. 7:22   B. 7:26   C. 7:36   D. 7:46

7. The MINIMUM headway shown on this schedule for a train leaving Deer St. is _____   7._____
minutes.

    A. 4   B. 6   C. 8   D. 10

8. The TOTAL number of trains stopping at Bay St. between 6:45 and 7:25 is   8._____

    A. 4   B. 6   C. 8   D. 10

9. The LONGEST travel time for a train elapses between _____ St. and _____ St.   9._____

    A. Wall; Ann   B. Ann; Deer
    C. Deer; Bay   D. Bay; Ellen

10. A train which arrives at Wall St. at 7:12 will next time arrive at Wall St. at   10._____

    A. 7:22   B. 8:08   C. 8:16   D. 8:24

KEY (CORRECT ANSWERS)

1.	C		6.	B
2.	B		7.	B
3.	D		8.	C
4.	B		9.	A
5.	C		10.	B

TEST 3

Questions 1-13.

DIRECTIONS: Questions 1 through 13 are to be answered SOLELY on the basis of the POR-TERS' WORK PROGRAMS shown below and the accompanying explanatory note.

CLEANERS' WORK PROGRAMS AT HUSTLE ST. STATION														
	#1 Tour of Duty 8 A.M. to 4 P.M.							#2 Tour of Duty 4 P.M. to Midnight						
Jobs To Be Done	M	T	W	T	F	S	A	M	T	W	T	F	S	S
Sweep entrance & street stairways	X	X	X	X	X	X	X	X	X	X	X	X	X	X
Sweep interior stairways	X	X	X	X	X	X	X	X	X	X	X	X	X	X
Scrap interior stairways								X	X	X	X	X	X	X
Empty vending machine receptacles	X		X		X		X	X		X		X		
Clean toilets & porters' room		X		X	X			X		X		X		X
Disinfect toilets		X			X									
Dust benches, handrails, booths, etc.	X											X		
Clean columns										X				
Clean signs				X				X					X	
Clean booths														X
Bag paper	X		X		X		X	X		X		X		
Scrap station & toilets	X	X	X	X	X	X	X							

Explanatory Note: X indicates the day on which the job is to be done. For example: Clean columns on #2 tour on Wednesdays only.

1. The TOTAL number of jobs to be done as shown on this schedule is

    A. 5   B. 6   C. 12   D. 14

1.____

2. On Tour #1, the GREATEST number of jobs is scheduled to be done on

    A. Monday   B. Wednesday   C. Friday   D. Saturday

2.____

3. On Tour #2, the GREATEST number of jobs is scheduled to be done on

    A. Monday   B. Wednesday   C. Friday   D. Saturday

3.____

4. The number of jobs which are scheduled to be done twice every day is

    A. 1   B. 2   C. 3   D. 4

4.____

5. The number of jobs which are scheduled to be done once every day is

    A. 2   B. 3   C. 4   D. 5

5.____

6. The job which is scheduled to be done once on EACH tour during the week is

6.____

A. clean signs   B. clean booths
C. dust benches   D. disinfect toilets

7. The job which is scheduled to be done once during the week is

7.____

A. clean signs   B. clean booths
C. dust benches   D. disinfect toilets

8. The number of jobs which are scheduled to be done only once during the week is

8.____

A. 1   B. 2   C. 3   D. 4

9. During the week, the porter on Tour #1 is scheduled to clean toilets

9.____

A. twice   B. 3 times   C. 4 times   D. 7 times

10. Trash receptacles under chewing gum machines are to be emptied

10.____

A. 3 times a week   B. 4 times a week
C. every day   D. twice a day

11. The number of different jobs scheduled to be done on Thursdays is

11.____

A. 5   B. 6   C. 8   D. 10

12. Handrails should be dusted on Tour #2 on the same day as

12.____

A. vending machines receptacles are emptied
B. paper is bagged
C. toilets are cleaned
D. the station is scrapped

13. You can infer, after reading all the Jobs To Be Done, that *scrap interior stairway* means

13.____

A. sweep them   B. disinfect them
C. clean the handrails   D. pick up litter from them

KEY (CORRECT ANSWERS)

1.	C	6.	C
2.	A	7.	B
3.	D	8.	B
4.	B	9.	B
5.	D	10.	C
		11.	C
		12.	C
		13.	D

TEST 4

Questions 1-10.

DIRECTIONS: Questions 1 through 10 are to be answered SOLELY on the basis of the portion of a timetable shown below.

	NORTHBOUND					SOUTHBOUND			
Train No.	Hall St. Lv.	Ann St. Lv.	Best St. Lv.	Knob Ave. Arr.	Knob Ave. Lv.	Best St. Lv.	Ann St. Lv.	Hall St. Arr.	Hall St. Lv.
88	7:35	7:50	8:05	8:15	8:20	8:30	8:45	9:00	9:05
89	7:50	8:05	8:20	8:30	8:35	8:45	9:00	9:15	9:20
90	8:05	8:20	8:35	8:45	8:50	9:00	9:15	9:30	9:35
91	8:20	8:35	8:50	9:00	9:05	9:15	9:30	9:45	9:50
92	8:30	8:45	9:00	9:10	9:15	9:25	9:40	9:55	10:00
93	8:40	8:55	9:10	9:20	9:25	9:35	9:50	10:05	10:10
94	8:50	9:05	9:20	9:30	9:35	9:45	10:00	10:15	10:20
95	9:00	9:15	9:30	9:40	9:45	9:55	10:10	10:25	10:30
88	9:05	9:20	9:35	9:45	9:50	10:00	10:15	10:30	LU*
96	9:10	9:25	9:40	9:50	9:55	10:05	10:20	10:35	10:40
97	9:15	9:30	9:45	9:55	10:00	10:10	10:25	10:40	LU*
89	9:20	9:35	9:50	10:00	10:05	10:15	10:30	10:45	10:50

TIMETABLE - *HH* LINE - WEEKDAYS

NOTE: LU* means that the train is taken out of passenger service at the location where LU appears. Assume that the arrival times at Ann St. and Best St. are the same as the leaving times.

1. The TOTAL number of different train numbers listed in the portion of the timetable shown is

   A. 9   B. 10   C. 11   D. 12

   1.____

2. For Train No. 95, the average of the running times from Hall St. to Ann St., from Ann St. to Best St., and from Best St. to Knob Ave. is about _____ minutes.

   A. 12   B. 13   C. 14   D. 15

   2.____

3. A passenger leaving Hall St. on the 7:50 train is going to Knob Ave. to take care of some business.
   If his business takes a total of one hour, he can be back at Hall St. by about

   A. 8:50   B. 9:20   C. 10:15   D. 10:40

   3.____

4. A passenger reaching Ann St. at 9:17 to leave on a northbound train would expect to arrive at Knob Ave. at

   A. 9:35   B. 9:45   C. 9:50   D. 10:15

   4.____

5. The TOTAL number of trains for which two complete round-trips are shown in the timetable is

    A. 4   B. 3   C. 2   D. 1

5.____

6. A person reaching Best St. at 9:03 to board a southbound train would have to wait until

    A. 9:05   B. 9:10   C. 9:15   D. 9:20

6.____

7. The length of time required for any train to make the northbound run from Hall St. to Knob Ave. is _____ minutes.

    A. 40   B. 45   C. 50   D. 85

7.____

8. The length of time that trains are scheduled to remain at Hall St. is _____ minutes.

    A. *always* 5   B. *always* 10
    C. *always* 15   D. *either* 5 or 10

8.____

9. From the entries in the timetable, you can infer that the location near which there is MOST likely to be a subway yard to store trains is

    A. Ann St.   B. Best St.   C. Knob Ave.   D. Hall St.

9.____

10. For Train No. 91, the TOTAL length of time, including the 5-minute layover at Knob Ave., required for one roundtrip from Hall St. to Knob Ave. and return is _____ minutes.

    A. 80   B. 85   C. 90   D. 120

10.____

KEY (CORRECT ANSWERS)

1.	B	6.	C
2.	B	7.	A
3.	C	8.	A
4.	B	9.	D
5.	C	10.	B

TEST 5

Questions 1-14.

DIRECTIONS: Questions 1 through 14 are to be answered SOLELY on the basis of the portion of the EMPLOYEES' TIME SHEET shown on the following page. When answering these items, refer to this time sheet and the accompanying explanatory note. It contains all of the essential information required to determine the amount earned by each employee, and enough computations are made to show you the method for filling in the blank spaces in the timesheet. For your own convenience, you are advised to compute and fill in the blank spaces in your test before answering any of these items. Then answer each of the items in the usual way.

EMPLOYEES' TIME SHEET

	Pay No.	Name	Hourly Rate	Time Reporting Date	AM	PM	Time Leaving Date	AM	PM	Time Actually Worked	Time Overtime Credit	Pay due
REGULAR TIME	41	King	$15.60	2-2-	7:00		2-2-		3:00	8 hrs.	X	62.
	39	Lee	14.40	2-2-		11:00	2-3-	7:00			X	
	85	Mark	16.20	2-3-	7:00		2-3-		3:00		X	
	64	Narr	15.00	2-3-		3:00	2-3-		11:00		X	
	75	Orr	14.40	2-4-		3:00	2-4-		11:00		X	
	29	Peer	16.20	2-5-	7:00		2-5-		3:00		X	
	36	Ray	15.60	2-5-		11:00	2-6-	7:00			X	
	45	Sill	15.60	2-6-	7:00		2-6-		3:00		X	
	91	Tone	14.40	2-6-		3:00	2-6-		11:00		X	
OVERTIME	41	King	$15.60	2-2-		3:00	2-2-		5:00	2 hrs.	3 hrs.	23.
	39	Lee	14.40	2-3-	7:00		2-3-	8:20				
	85	Mark	16.20	2-3-		3:00	2-3-		3:40			
	64	Narr	15.00	2-3-		11:00	2-3-		11:40			
	75	Orr	14.40	2-4-		11:00	2-5-	12:20				
	29	Peer	16.20	2-5-		3:00	2-5-		3:20			
	36	Ray	15.60	2-6-	7:00		2-6-	8:00				
	45	Sill	15.60	2-6-		3:00	2-6-		4:20			
	91	Tone	14.40	2-6-		11: 00	2-7-	12:40				

NOTE: All overtime credit is at the rate of time and one-half.

1. On February 3, Mark should be credited for both regular time and overtime with a total of _____ hours _____ minutes.

    A. 8; 40   B. 9; 0   C. 9; 20   D. 9; 40

1._____

2. The individuals listed on the time sheet are designated by

    A. pay numbers   B. hourly rates   C. overtime rates D. dates

2._____

3. The difference between the maximum and the minimum hourly rates of pay as shown in the table is

    A. 60¢   B. $1.20   C. $1.80   D. $2.40

3._____

4. The man earning the LARGEST amount for overtime (of the following) was   4.____

    A. Sill   B. Tone   C. Lee   D. Orr

5. The man who earned $16.20 for base pay was   5.____

    A. Narr   B. Mark   C. Orr   D. Ray

6. The number of men entitled to less than 9 hours pay was   6.____

    A. 1   B. 2   C. 3   D. 4

7. Of the following, the man who put in the LEAST overtime was   7.____

    A. Lee   B. King   C. Narr   D. Orr

8. The two men earning the SMALLEST amount for overtime were   8.____

    A. Narr and Peer   B. Narr and Mark
    C. Mark and Ray   D. Ray and Peer

9. The table shows that more men were needed for overtime at _____ than at _____ .   9.____

    A. 7:00 A.M.; 3:00 P.M.   B. 7:00 A.M.; 11:00 P.M.
    C. 11:00 P.M.; 3:00 A.M.   D. 11:00 P.M.; 7:00 A.M.

10. If Peer's overtime was due to the late arrival of his relief who is paid at the hourly rate of $14.40, then the extra cost to the Transit Authority was   10.____

    A. 90¢   B. $1.10   C. $1.80   D. $3.30

11. On February 3, the man earning the LARGEST amount for overtime was   11.____

    A. Lee   B. Mark   C. Narr   D. Orr

12. On February 6, Sill's pay for overtime was _____ of his total earnings.   12.____

    A. 15%   B. 20%   C. 25%   D. 30%

13. On February 6, Ray received a total pay of   13.____

    A. $124.80   B. $132.60   C. $140.40   D. $148.20

14. On February 3, the total cost for overtime was   14.____

    A. $31.20   B. $43.80   C. $45.00   D. $60.00

KEY (CORRECT ANSWERS)

1. B	6. A	11. A	
2. A	7. C	12. B	
3. C	8. A	13. D	
4. B	9. D	14. D	
5. B	10. D		

TEST 6

Questions 1-11.

DIRECTIONS: Questions 1 through 11 are to be answered SOLELY on the basis of the timetable shown below and the accompanying notes.

TIMETABLE - CROSSTOWN LINE LOCALS WEEKDAYS WITHOUT SATURDAY											
NORTHBOUND						SOUTHBOUND					
Cable St.	Fail St.	Duke Pl.	Gain St.	Lack Ave.		Gain St.	Duke Pl.		Fail St.	Cable St.	
Lv.	Lv.	Lv.	Lv.	Arr.	Lv.	Lv.	Arr.	Lv.	Lv.	Arr.	Lv.
P7:20	7:35	7:48	7:58	8:12	8:18	8:32	-	8:42	8:55	9:10	9:20
-	-	P7:52	8:02	8:16	8:22	8:36	8:46	8:52	-	-	-
7:28	7:43	7:56	8:06	8:20	8:26	8:40	-	8:50	9:03	9:18	9:28
-	-	8:00	8:10	8:24	8:30	8:44	8:54	9:00	-	-	-
7:36	7:51	8:04	8:14	8:28	8:34	8:48	-	8:58	9:11	9:26	9:38
-	-	8:08	8:18	8:32	8:38	8:52	9:02	9:10	-	-	-
P7:44	7:59	8:12	8:22	8:36	8:42	8:56	-	9:06	9:19	9:34	L
-	-	P8:16	8:26	8:40	8:46	9:00	9:10	9:20	-	-	-
7:52	8:07	8:20	8:30	8:44	8:50	9:04	-	9:14	9:27	9:42	9:48
-	-	8:23	X	8:47	8:53	9:07	9:17	L	-	-	-
7:58	8:13	8:26	8:36	8:50	8:56	9:10	-	9:20	9:33	9:48	9:58
-	-	8:29	8:39	8:53	8:59	9:13	9:23	9:30	-	-	-
P8:04	8:19	8:32	8:42	8:56	9:02	9:16	-	9:26	9:39	9:54	L
-	-	8:35	8:45	8:59	9:05	9:19	9:29	9:40	-	-	-
8:10	8:25	8:38	8:48	9:02	9:08	9:22	-	9:32	9:45	10:00	10:08
-	-	P8:41	8:51	9:05	9:11	9:25	9:35	L	-	-	-
8:16	8:31	8:44	8:54	9:08	9:14	9:28	-	9:38	9:51	10:06	10:18
-	-	8:47	8:57	9:11	9:17	9:31	9:41	9:50	-	-	-
8:22	8:37	8:50	9:00	9:14	9:20	9:34	-	9:44	9:57	10:12	L
-	-	8:52	9:02	9:16	9:22	9:36	9:46	L	-	-	-
8:26	8:41	8:54	9:04	9:18	9:24	9:38	-	9:48	10:01	10:16	10:28
-	-	P8:56	9:06	9:20	9:26	9:40	9:50	10:00	-	-	-
P8:30	8:45	8:58	9:08	9:22	9:28	9:42	-	9:52	10:05	10:20	L

NOTES: 1. P denotes that a train is placed in passenger service where the letter P
appears.
2. L denotes that a train is taken out of passenger service where the letter L
appears.

1.   The TOTAL number of scheduled roundtrips between Cable St. and Lack Ave. during the
period shown is

1._____

        A. 8   B. 12   C. 19   D. 23

2. The scheduled running time between Cable St. and Lack Ave. is _____ minutes.   2._____

    A. 48   B. 52   C. 58   D. 90

3. The number of trains which are laid up after making one roundtrip from Cable St. is   3._____

    A. 1   B. 2   C. 3   D. 4

4. The number of trains which are laid up after making one roundtrip from Duke Pl. is   4._____

    A. 1   B. 2   C. 3   D. 4

5. Before 9:00, there is a train leaving Lack Ave. every _____ minutes.   5._____

    A. 2 or 3   B. 3   C. 4   D. 3or4

6. After 9:00, there is a train leaving Lack Ave. every _____ minutes.   6._____

    A. 2   B. 2 or 3   C. 3   D. 3or4

7. The train which is put in at Duke St. at 7:52 is scheduled to lay up after its second   7._____
   roundtrip at

    A. 8:52   B. 9:44   C. 9:46   D. 9:48

8. The timetable indicates that a number of storage tracks or a yard is located near   8._____

    A. Gain St.   B. Fail St.   C. Duke Pl.   D. Lack Ave.

9. If a passenger arrives on the Gain St. Station at 9:00, he can expect to get to Cable St. at   9._____

    A. 9:48   B. 9:42   C. 9:34   D. 9:27

10. The number marked X which has been omitted from the leaving column at Gain St. is   10._____

    A. 8:32   B. 8:33   C. 8:34   D. 8:35

11. Assuming that the headway leaving Cable St. southbound does not change after 10:28,   11._____
    the train which is scheduled to leave NEAREST Noon is scheduled to leave Cable St. at

    A. 11:46   B. 11:48   C. 11:58   D. 12:08

KEY (CORRECT ANSWERS)

1.	B	6.	B
2.	B	7.	C
3.	C	8.	C
4.	A	9.	B
5.	D	10.	B

11. C

TEST 7

Questions 1-8.

DIRECTIONS: Questions 1 through 8 are to be answered SOLELY on the basis of the portion of the ARRIVAL TIMETABLE for Bay St. local station of the subway shown below. This table shows the times when trains are scheduled to arrive at Bay St. Station. Refer to this timetable, and consider only the period of time covered by the table when answering these questions.

ARRIVAL TIMETABLE							
SOUTHBOUND				NORTHBOUND			
Col. 1	Col. 2	Col. 3	Col. 4	Col. 5	Col. 6	Col. 7	Col. 8
Mon. PM to Fri. AM	Fri. PM to Sat. AM	Sat. PM to Sun. AM	Sun. PM to Mon. AM	Mon. PM to Fri. AM	Fri. PM to Sat. AM	Sat. PM to Sun. AM	Sun. PM to Mon. AM
11:42	11:42	11:42	11:44	11:44	11:44	11:25	11:44
11:54	11:52	11:52	11:54	11:54	11:54	11:33	11:54
12:06	12:02	12:02	12:06	12:04	12:04	11:41	12:04
12:18	12:12	12:12	12:18	12:14	12:14	11:49	12:14
12:30	12:22	12:22	12:30	.12:24	12:24	11:57	12:24
12:42	12:34	12:32	12:42	12:34	12:34	12:05	12:34
12:54	12:46	12:42	12:54	12:46	12:44	12:15	12:46
1:09	12:58	12:52	1:09	12:58	12:54	12:25	12:58
1:24	1:13	1:02	1:24	1:10	1:04	12:35	1:10
1:44	1:28	1:14	1:44	1:22	1:14	12:45	1:22
2:04	1:41	1:26	2:04	1:34	1:24	12:55	1:34
2:24	1:56	1:38	2:24	1:46	1:34	1:05	1:46

1. Two columns which show exactly the SAME arrival time for every train are Columns _____ and _____ .

    A.   1; 3   B.   2; 4   C.   5; 8   D.   6; 7

1.____

2. The number of nights per week to which Column 1 applies is

    A.   5   B.   4   C.   3   D.   1

2.____

3. The TOTAL number of northbound trains scheduled to arrive at Bay St. Station from 12:45 A.M. to 1:15 A.M. on Tuesday is

    A.   5   B.   3   C.   2   D.   1

3.____

4. The TOTAL number of all trains scheduled to arrive at this station between 11:45 P.M. Friday and 1:30 A.M. Saturday is

    A.   9   B.   10   C.   19   D.   21

4.____

5. A northbound train is due at this station at 12:34 A.M. every day of the week EXCEPT
   5.____

    A. Friday   B. Saturday   C. Sunday   D. Monday

6. A passenger who wants to get a northbound train anytime after 11:59 P.M. on Wednes-
   day can tell from the timetable that the MAXIMUM length of time he must wait for the next
   train if he just misses one is _____ minutes.
   6.____

    A. 15   B. 12   C. 10   D. 8

7. The TOTAL time elapsed from the first to the last train of Column 6 is_____ hours
   _____ minutes.
   7.____

    A. 2; 10   B. 2; 30   C. 1; 50   D. 1; 10

8. If a passenger who wishes to board a southbound train arrives on Bay St. platform at
   Midnight on Saturday, he can expect to board a train at
   8.____

    A. 12:06   B. 12:05   C. 12:04   D. 12:02

KEY (CORRECT ANSWERS)

1.	C	5.	C
2.	B	6.	B
3.	B	7.	C
4.	C	8.	D